A Pocket Book on

Pure Food

Healthy eating without additives

Recipes by Marie Green and
Pauline Hemmings

Edited by Jenni Fleetwood

Octopus Books

A Pocket Book on

Pure Food

Healthy eating without additives

Recipes by Marie Green and
Pauline Hemmings

Edited by Jenni Fleetwood
Introduced by Jenny Salmon, MSc

Octopus Books

Contents

Introduction	4
Breakfasts	30
Starters	38
Stocks and Soups	42
Vegetables and Salads	46
Pulses and Pasta	54

First published 1985 by
Octopus Books Limited
59 Grosvenor Street
London W1

ISBN 0 7064 2311 9

Produced by Mandarin Publishers Ltd
22a Westlands Road, Quarry Bay,
Hong Kong

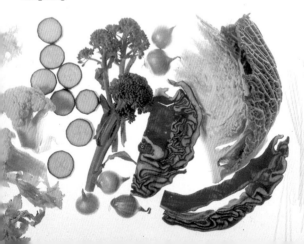

Sauces	59
Meat, Fish and Poultry Dishes	66
Baking	75
Drinks	82
Home-made 'Convenience Foods'	86
Index	95

Introduction

For many years now there has been growing unease over the possible excessive use of food additives. More and more people are reading food labels and selecting those foods with the shortest list of added chemicals. Consumers are beginning to question not only what effects chemicals, such as monosodium glutamate, butylated hydroxyanisole and tartrazine and so on, may be having on their bodies, but why they are added to food in the first place. After all, they are not the ingredients you find in cookery books.

The exhortations of the scientists about the safety of these compounds do little to quell anxiety and any concerned consumer would simply prefer their food to be as free of the 'hidden extras' as possible.

What are food additives?

Clearly, it isn't easy to give a precise definition of a food additive. The Food Labelling Regulations (1980) define an additive as 'any substance not commonly regarded or used as food, which is added to, or used in or on food at any stage to affect its keeping quality, texture, consistency, taste, odour, alkalinity or acidity, or to serve any other technological function in relation to food, and including processing aids in so far as they are added to, or used in or on food'.

If asked for examples of food additives, most people will usually mention preservatives, colourings and artificial flavourings; a few will recognise the terms anti-oxidants, emulsifiers and flavour-enhancers. But what exactly are all these chemicals and why are they added to our food?

Preservatives and anti-oxidants extend a food's 'shelf-life' — they enable foods to be distributed to supermarkets, stored at home and eaten weeks, or even months later.

Nitrates and Nitrites inhibit the growth of micro-organisms which may render food unpalatable or poisonous or both.

Stabilizers ensure that the texture of foods, especially sauces, is not altered during distribution and storage, and that they remain attractive.

Emulsifiers help prevent sauces and other processed foods from separating.

Obviously the effects of these food additives are largely beneficial. If they weren't used, everybody, from the manufacturer to the consumer, would have to be far more careful about the length of storage time, and the conditions under which the foods are stored.

Colourings and flavourings on the other hand, are not essential but they are used to add appeal to foods. Without colours and flavours, some of today's convenience foods would either not exist or would simply not be popular.

There is a great deal of truth in the statement 'we eat with our eyes'. The colour of food often affects the way we perceive flavour. Experiment and prove it to yourself. Take one sweet from a packet of mixed flavours without first looking to see what colour it is. Eat it. Can you tell if it is strawberry, raspberry, lemon, orange or lime-flavoured? The chances are you can't. Experiments show that if a raspberry-flavoured food is coloured yellow, the majority of people will think they are eating a lemon-flavoured food. Where the flavours of manufactured foods are indistinct, we shouldn't be surprised that the food manufacturer feels he must add artificial colour and flavour to help our taste buds identify what we are eating.

Synthetic versus natural additives

Most people believe that the chemicals added to food — whether they preserve, colour, or flavour the food — are chemicals that have been manufactured in the laboratory but often this is not the case. Some additives originate in the laboratory, but others are extracted from plants.

Carotene, a yellow colouring agent, can be produced in the laboratory or extracted from foods such as carrots and dark green vegetables. Lecithin is an emulsifier found in many foods, notably eggs. (We rely upon its emulsifying properties when combining oil and vinegar in the making of mayonnaise.) Lecithin is extracted from foods such as seaweed and used in commercially prepared foods. The label will show 'lecithin' in the ingredients panel, and, strictly speaking, it is an additive.

However, the fact that an additive is produced from a natural food substance is no guarantee that it is healthy. Nucleotides are an essential part of the nucleus of every living cell, the basis of the genetic material that is handed on from generation to generation in all living things. These nucleotides are extracted from organisms such as yeasts and used as flavourings. Being a natural substance it could be regarded as 'safe'. There is, however, a theory that vast quantities of nucleotides, absorbed over a period of many years, may be the cause of uric acid kidney stones, gout and some cases of arthritis.

It is reassuring to know that the body can deal with small quantities of practically any chemical without harm and it is worth remembering that practically any substance can be dangerous to our health if we eat enough of it. Small amounts of common salt are essential to normal health, a little too much may help to cause high blood pressure in some people and an excess will certainly kill you. Nutmeg, if used too freely, can cause hallucinations. Inadequately cooked red kidney beans contain an alkaloid which, in very large doses, can poison you.

But we go on eating reasonable amounts of salt, nutmeg, and kidney beans without giving their contents a thought. And mostly they do us nothing but good. So whether something is good or bad for us depends largely on how much of it we eat. What may be fine in small doses may be anything but fine in larger amounts.

Flavour and colour can be lost during the canning process so additives may be added to compensate.

Both the government and food industry claim that the tests they carry out satisfactorily prove the safety of additives.

Quantity and control

No one is able to tell us for certain the number of food additives we consume nor the quantity, but it is thought on average a person will consume anything from 3 to 7 kg (6-15 lb) each year. This figure varies considerably depending upon a person's diet; a teenager who consumes large quantities of prepackaged snack foods and fizzy drinks will consume far more additives than a person who eats mainly simple, home prepared dishes.

Just over 300 food additives are regulated and monitored by government agencies, yet this is only about one-tenth of the 3,500 food additives used by the food industry. This means that there could be as many as 3,000 different chemicals being added to our food and drink which are not being fully tested. Flavourings, starches and enzymes are the least regulated of all groups of additives.

Since 1983, nearly all packaged foods have had to carry a list of ingredients including additives. (Exceptions include certain sugar products, cocoa and chocolate products, honey, milk and certain condensed and dried milk products, hen's eggs, coffee and coffee products.)

Some groups of additives have to be declared by their generic name and either their specific name or a number allocated by the EEC – their E number. So, tartrazine can appear either as 'Colouring – tartrazine' or 'Colouring – E 102'. There are additives which do not, as yet, have E numbers, but some of these simply have a number without the E prefix. These are numbers which are not recognised by the EEC but which have been allocated by the UK authorities. A complete list of regulated additives together with their serial numbers can be obtained from the Ministry of Agriculture, Fisheries and Food in their booklet, *Look at the Label,* (see page 16).

Insecticides and sprays

There are also the 'additives' that are *not* listed on food packets. Most fruit, vegetables and cereals are sprayed with chemicals to prevent insects and micro-organisms causing rot and diseases, and with fertilisers to increase vegetable yields. Strictly speaking these are additives that are cause for concern but you certainly won't find them labelled in the greengrocer's shop. The best precaution you can take against the effects of insecticides and sprays, is to scrub fruit and vegetables thoroughly in water before you use them. It is important to do this whether or not you are going to peel the skins.

The testing of food additives

Those additives that are controlled by the Government are subjected to extensive tests. Obviously, it is not ethical to test food additives on humans so the main tests to assess safety are carried out on animals. But this can never be regarded as completely satisfactory unless we know whether the metabolism of the animals tested is comparable to ours. In other words, do additives behave in the same way, for example, in a rat's body as they do in a human body?

Moreover, who is to say that all humans are able to metabolize additives in the same way? It is likely that people's ability to metabolize specific additives will vary considerably, with some people reacting adversely to a substance that has no effect on the majority of the population. Why else do some people develop a rash or headache when they eat strawberries or shell fish, when most of us can eat them with no adverse reactions?

Adverse effects of food additives

Despite the government's confidence in the testing procedures used, there is growing evidence that some accepted food additives may have adverse effects on some people.

Allergies

Allergic reactions attributed to additives range from skin rashes and runny nose, to asthma, arthritis, stomach pain and depression, hyperactivity in children and mental disorders in adults. The table on page 10 gives some common additives and their alleged adverse effects.

Obviously attempting to discover whether someone is allergic to a specific food additive can be a very time-consuming exercise, but there is a well-established procedure to follow. Firstly the suspected allergen is placed on the skin or inhaled and the patient's reaction is noted. The blood can also be analysed for antibodies and if a particular type of antibody is found, the person is suspected to be allergic to that substance. Then the suspect food or additive is withheld for a few days, or sometimes for much longer. If the patient's symptoms disappear, that is further evidence of allergy. The final test is to challenge the person with the suspected food or additive. If the original symptoms re-appear, the allergy and its cause have been proved.

Many allegations that foods and food additives cause allergic reactions are not based on the tests outlined above, but on highly subjective observations. It's very easy for an investigator to 'imagine' a particular response if he is expecting it. Equally, if the patient thinks his 'treatment' will work he is quite likely to show an improvement, even if he is, in fact, receiving no treatment at all.

But in spite of this general lack of proof about the adverse effects of food additives, there are some quite well-known cases where an additive can have ill-effects and other cases where there is suspicion but no proof yet.

Some common additives and their alleged effects

Additive:	Found in:	Alleged effects:
E102 Tartrazine, a yellow azo dye	Fizzy drinks, pie fillings, cheese rind, tinned peas, sweets, mint sauce, yellow foods	Asthma, migraine, hyperactivity in children
E110 Sunset Yellow FCF, a coal dye	Orange squash, lemon curd, packet soup mix, hot chocolate	Skin rashes, swollen blood vessels
E124 Ponceau 4R, a synthetic red dye	Packet trifle, tinned straw-berries and strawberry milk shake, dessert topping, soup mixes, quick setting jelly mix	Aggravates asthma
E142 Lissamine Green, a synthetic green dye	Gravy granules, mint jelly, tinned peas, packet breadcrumbs	Aggravates eczema and asthma
E151 Black PN, a synthetic black dye	Blackcurrant pie filling, brown sauce	Aggravates hypertension
Nitrates and nitrites	Smoked foods	Some cancers, methaemoglo-binaemia in babies and very young children
Monosodium glutamate	Soy sauce and much Chinese food	Dizziness, headaches, burning skin

Above: *Fruit trees being sprayed against insects and disease. Most fruit is sprayed in this way, but it rarely carries a label to say so, though it is often possible to detect a powdery white film on the surface of fruit you have just bought. It is always advisable to wash all fruit thoroughly before you eat it.*
Below: *The colours and flavourings in many prepacked cakes contribute nothing to the nutritional content. Avoid them by making your own with fresh, natural ingredients.*

The number of people affected
When it comes to finding out how many people have adverse reactions to food additives, the matter becomes difficult. Research undertaken by different investigators has produced widely varying results. One experiment on patients with urticaria (itchy skin rash) showed a reaction in 33% of the patients to one or more additives, while in another test the figure was 50%. In one case tartrazine produced a reaction in 5% of people tested, in another case, 46%.

These tests were all done on sensitive people. In the population at large it is estimated that as many as six people in every 10,000 may be allergic to the colouring tartrazine and at least one in 1,000 may react to preservatives such as benzoates. Overall, the EEC has estimated that between three and fifteen people in 10,000 may be allergic to one or more food additives.

Hyperactivity and cancer
The above figures, that in theory reflect the number of people who may be allergic to food additives, are extremely low, but they relate only to food allergy and other forms of food intolerance. What they don't deal with is a matter of far greater concern: the effect any additive may have on the incidence of hyperactivity and cancers. That is much more difficult to assess.

Tartrazine and other azo dyes Tartrazine is a yellow colouring used in many foods including orange drinks and the 'golden' crumbs on products such as fish fingers. It is a member of the azo group of colourings. Others with a similar chemical structure include Amaranth, Ponceau 4R, Sunset Yellow and Brown FK. Tartrazine's most widely publicised adverse effect, allegedly, is hyperactivity in children. As a result of research in the USA in the early 1970s a Dr Feingold claimed that many over-active children who were difficult to control and who found it hard to concentrate could be 'cured' if they ate a diet free from tartrazine and other colourings, preservatives and salicylates. (Salicylates occur naturally in cucumbers and in fruits such as apples, oranges, tomatoes and berries.)

When medical authorities in the USA carried out trials to

find out if this additive-free diet worked they concluded that it was, in fact, ineffective. They claimed that any beneficial effect it might have had in some children was merely due to observer bias. In other words, parents and teachers wanted and expected an improvement so they imagined that the children were more controllable. However, there is evidence that children under the age of about five years do benefit from a diet which is free from additives and naturally occurring salicylates.

Nitrates and nitrites Nitrates and nitrites are used to preserve foods – mainly meats and fish – by preventing the growth of micro-organisms, including the highly dangerous *Clostridium botulinum*. Nitrites are also essential to the process whereby pork is cured to produce ham and bacon.

There is a considerable amount of evidence that nitrates can be converted to nitrites and these can in turn combine with another group of chemicals known as amines to form nitrosamines. It is known that this group of chemical compounds can cause stomach cancer. But the production of nitrosamines is inhibited by vitamin C and by temperatures in the region of 2°C. So that's a good reason for taking plenty of citrus fruits and juices and for storing food in the refrigerator. It's important, too, to look at the role of nitrates and nitrites as food additives in perspective. Only about 10% of our total daily intake of them comes from 'additive' nitrates and nitrites. The rest comes from drinking water and vegetables via fertilisers. However, the conclusive evidence of their relation to stomach cancer should be sufficient reason for us to cut down on the amount of smoked foods and other nitrate and nitrite containing foods we consume.

Monosodium glutamate

The additive we all love to hate, monosodium glutamate (MSG), is probably the best known and the most controversial of all food additives. It is a flavour enhancer, very widely used in prepared foods. Almost flavourless itself it is capable of enhancing the flavour of a great many meat, fish and cheese dishes. It is, in fact, a slightly modified version of glutamic acid, one of the amino acids from which body proteins are made. It sounds harmless enough; if we didn't have any glutamic acid in our bodies we could not make our own body proteins. However, eating a virtually pure amino acid, no matter which one it is, is very different from eating amino acids in the form of proteins. So don't be tempted to buy it from the health food shops because it won't do you any good.

Soy sauce is an extremely rich source of MSG and Chinese dishes and those foods which contain liberal quantities of soy sauce are likely to contain far more MSG than typically British dishes. Some people are sensitive to MSG and find that after they have eaten a Chinese meal well-laced with soy sauce they feel dizzy, have headaches and feel a burning sensation on the skin. The symptoms pass fairly quickly and seem to have no lasting effect. However, tests with animals are reported to show brain damage when very large amounts are consumed. But against this it is comforting to know that the Chinese – lifelong consumers of large amounts of MSG – do not have a higher incidence of brain damage than any other population. Still, there is no doubt that some people are sensitive to MSG and the best thing they can do is to avoid eating large amounts of it.

So are food additives safe?

According to the food industry and government food additives are subjected to sufficiently rigorous controls before manufacturers are allowed to use them. The truth is, however, that although many additives are tested, the majority are not. Most groups, such as colourings and emulsifiers are controlled by having a 'permitted list', but there is no 'permitted list' of flavourings.

Work still goes on to evaluate the long-term effect that food additives may have on our bodies both on their own and in combinations with other substances usually found in foods and there is evidence that some additives can have an adverse effect on some people.

It is important to remember that far more ill-health is caused by eating a poorly balanced diet, by food poisoning, by smoking cigarettes, by not taking enough physical exercise and by naturally occurring toxins in food than by food additives. But since it is impossible to say that all additives are safe to all people and since so many of those chemicals used by the food industry are under investigation it does make sense for you to reduce the number of food additives you and your family consume.

Reducing the food additives in your diet

If you know you or a member of your family have a specific adverse reaction to one particular additive you will need to be able to identify individual additives, discover to which foods they are added and attempt to eliminate these from your diet.

If, however, your interest is directed towards cutting your additive intake in general, concentrate on cutting colourings, flavourings and emulsifiers rather than on preservatives. These are all more important to the appearance and taste of food than to its nutritional value and keeping qualities so they can all be easily dispensed with. (There are ways, after all, for manufacturers to prepare food, which do not require the addition of colouring and flavouring.)

Foods that are high in food additives tend to be the 'convenience' or 'snack' type and by avoiding such foods you are not only reducing the number of additives you consume, but you are also likely to improve the nutritional quality of your diet. You will be cutting out sweet and savoury between-meal snacks and eating far more home-cooked dishes.

Foods cooked at home from natural ingredients are likely to contain far fewer additives than those bought canned, chilled or frozen. When selecting ingredients for home use, read the label of the food before buying it and always opt for the product with the least number of added chemicals.

The ingredients used in this book are not expensive or quirky health foods. They are wholesome, everyday ingredients that are low in added chemicals. The recipes that follow show how easy and quick it is to prepare nutritionally balanced dishes using these ingredients. The meals created from these recipes will be just as appealing to your family as highly processed, convenience foods, but are likely to be far lower in additives and far higher in nutrients. For the sake of your family's health, try some and see.

Read the label
The following table gives a selection of the additives and serial numbers listed in the Ministry of Agriculture, Foods and Fisheries' leaflet *Look at the Label*. These are among the additives most commonly found in our daily diet. We also list some of the foods in which they are used, as well as the functions they perform.

Colours
E101 Riboflavin (Lactoflavin, Vitamin B_2)
A naturally occurring ingredient used to add yellow colour and Vitamin B_2 to processed cheese.
E102 Tartrazine
A synthetic yellow dye (see page 10), used in many packet convenience foods.
E104 Quinoline Yellow
A synthetic dye which is used as a food colouring in products such as scotch eggs and smoked haddock.
107 Yellow 2G
A synthetic dye without an EEC prefix yet, used as a food colour.
E110 Sunset Yellow FCF (Orange Yellow S) (see page 10)
A synthetic dye used in sweets, orange squash, apricot jam and lemon curd.
E122 Carmoisine (Azorubine)
A synthetic dye used to add red colour to packet soups, packet breadcrumbs, packet cheesecake mixes and packet jellies.
E123 Amaranth
Another red dye used in packet cake and trifle mixes.
E124 Ponceau 4R (Cochineal Red A)
A synthetic red dye used in canned cherry, redcurrant and raspberry fillings.
E127 Erythrosine BS
A synthetic dye used in sausages and cooked meat products.
E132 Indigo Carmine (Indigotine)
A synthetic blue dye used in sweets and biscuits.
E140 Chlorophyll
A naturally occurring green colour found in nettles and grass and used in fats, oils and fruits that are preserved in liquid.

Preservatives
E200 Sorbic acid
A naturally occurring substance which can also be manufactured synthetically, it is used in sweets, soft drinks, packet cake topping and sweet sauces.
E201 Sodium sorbate
A naturally occurring preservative used in frozen pizzas.
E202 Potassium sorbate
A manufactured antifungal preservative used in margarine, salad dressing and prepacked cakes.
E210 Benzoic acid
Naturally occurring but also manufactured, it is used to preserve jam, pickles, beer and salad dressing, and is found in marinated herring.
E211 Sodium benzoate
Made from benzoic acid, this is used to preserve fruit pies, barbecue sauce, and packet cheesecake mixes.
E214 Ethyl 4-hydroxybenzoate
Made from benzoic acid, this is used to preserve jams, fruit sauces and crystallised fruits.
E216 Propyl 4-hydroxybenzoate
Produced from benzoic acid this is used as a preservative in prepacked cooked beetroot, fruit purées and pickles.
E218 Methyl 4-hydroxybenzoate
A synthetic preservative used in snack meals and concentrated soups.
E220 Sulphur dioxide
Occurring naturally but manufactured for use in products such as packet soups, blackcurrant jam, canned cauliflower and sausage meat.
E223 Sodium metabisulphite
A synthetic preservative used in packet mashed potato and orange squash.
E230 Biphenyl (Diphenyl)
A synthetic antifungal agent used on the skins of oranges and lemons
E231 2 Hydroxybiphenyl (Orthophenylphenol)
A synthetic preservative used on the skins of oranges, lemons and limes.
E250 Sodium nitrite
A sodium derivative used in cured meat, smoked frankfurters and pressed meat.

E251 Sodium nitrate
A natural substance used to preserve bacon, ham, cheese and frozen pizzas.
E252 Potassium nitrate
Artificially manufactured for use as a curing salt in meats and sausages.
E262 Sodium hydrogen diacetate
A synthetic preservative used in shaped crisps.
E270 Lactic acid
A natural substance used in margarines and bottled cheese spreads.

Anti-oxidants
E300 L-Ascorbic acid (Vitamin C)
A naturally occurring vitamin, added to fresh, cut fruits to inhibit browning.
E301 Sodium L-ascorbic acid
A synthetic salt prepared from ascorbic acid and used as an anti-oxidant and colour preservative in sausages, scotch eggs and frankfurters.
E302 Calcium L-ascorbate
A synthetic anti-oxidant used in scotch eggs.
E304 6-0-Palmitoyl-L-ascorbic acid (Ascorbyl palmitate)
A synthetic anti-oxidant and colour preservative used in chicken stock cubes.
E306 Extracts of natural origin rich in tocopherols
(Vitamin E)
Used in packet dessert toppings to add Vitamin E and as an anti-oxidant.
E307 Synthetic *alpha*-tocopherol
Synthetic Vitamin E used in sausages.
E308 Synthetic *gamma*-tocopherol
Origin and function as above.
E309 Synthetic *delta*-tocopherol
Origin and function as above.
E310 Propyl gallate
A synthetically prepared anti-oxidant which is used in some breakfast cereals, as well as instant potato and snack foods.
E311 Octyl gallate
A synthetically prepared anti-oxidant, which is not used in foods intended for babies or young children.

E312 Dodecyl gallate
Another synthetically prepared anti-oxidant.
E320 Butylated hydroxyanisole (BHA)
A synthetically prepared anti-oxidant used in biscuits, sweets, beef stock cubes and in savoury rice.
E321 Butylated hydroxytolene (BHT)
A synthetically prepared anti-oxidant used in packet cake mixes, crisps, gravy granules and breakfast cereals.

Emulsifiers, Stabilizers and Others
E322 Lecithins
Naturally occurring emulsifiers (see page 5), used in dessert packet mixes, margarines and chocolate biscuits.
E325 Sodium lactate
Derived from lactic acid, this is used to prevent loss of moisture in confectionery and cheese.
E330 Citric acid
Naturally occurring in citrus fruits but also prepared commercially, it is used in canned vegetables, frozen potatoes, jams, jellies and ice cream. It acts as a flavouring agent as well as preventing discoloration in fresh fruit.
E331 Sodium dihydrogen citrate (*mono*Sodium citrate, *tri*Sodium citrate)
Sodium salts prepared from citric acid, which can be used to stimulate the action of other anti-oxidants. Used in ice cream and sweets.
E332 Potassium dihydrogen citrate (*mono*Potassium citrate), *di*Potassium citrate, *tri*Potassium citrate
Potassium salts which are prepared from citric acid and used as emulsifiers and anti-oxidants in some crisps and dessert packet mixes.
E333 *Mono, di* and *tri* Calcium citrate
Calcium salts prepared from citric acid and used as emulsifiers in fizzy drinks and cheeses.
E334 L-(+)-Tartaric acid
Grapes are the natural source of tartaric acid. It is manufactured for use in jams, jellies and marmalades as an anti-oxidant.
E336 *Mono*Potassium L-(+)-tartrate (Cream of tartar)
Produced from tartaric acid, it is commonly used as a raising agent in baking, but also as an emulsifier. Used in lemon meringue packet mixes.

E337 Potassium sodium L-(+)-tartrate
Prepared from tartaric acid and used to stimulate the action of anti-oxidants in meat and cheese products.

385 Calcium disodium ethylenediamine-NNN'N' tetra-acetate (Calcium disodium EDTA)
A synthetically prepared chemical used to stabilize the ingredients in salad dressing.

E400 Alginic acid
A naturally occurring substance found in some seaweeds and used as a gelling agent in instant desserts.

E401 Sodium alginate
Prepared from alginic acid, this is used as an emulsifier in barbecue sauce mixes, packet cheesecake mixes and canned fruit pie fillings.

E405 Propane-1,2-diol alginate
Manufactured from alginic acid and used in prepared mint sauce and salad dressings.

E406 Agar
A natural substance derived from some seaweeds. It is used as a thickening agent in ice cream and meat glazes.

E407 Carrageenan
Naturally occurring in some seaweeds. It is used as an emulsifier and a gelling agent in milk shake mixes, jelly mixes and salad dressings.

E410 Locust bean gum (Carob gum)
Derived from the Carob tree and used to stabilize the ingredients in canned fruit pie fillings and salad cream.

E412 Guar gum
A natural gum used in brown sauce, piccalilli, sauce tartare and milk shakes.

E415 Xanthan gum
A stabilizer found in salad dressings, horseradish sauce and sweet pickle.

E416 Karaya gum
A natural gum used as a thickener in savoury sauces.

E420 Sorbitol, sorbitol syrup
A naturally occurring sugar alcohol that is also manufactured. It is used as a sweetening agent and found in chocolates, pastries and prepacked cakes.

E421 Mannitol
A naturally occurring sugar prepared from some seaweeds. It is used as a sweetener and an anti-caking agent.

E422 Glycerol
A naturally occurring sweetener used in cake icing and confectionery

430 Polyoxyethylene (8) Stearate
A manufactured emulsifier used in breads and cakes.

434 Polyoxyethylene (20) sorbitan monopalmitate
Prepared from sorbitol and used for its stabilizing and emulsifying properties.

E440(a) Pectin
A water soluble carbohydrate, naturally occurring in ripe fruits. Used as a gelling agent in jams and marmalade.

E440(b) Amidated pectin
Produced from pectin and used in jams and jellies.

442 Ammonium phosphatides
A synthetic emulsifier used in products containing cocoa and chocolate.

E460 Microcrystalline cellulose, *Alpha*-cellulose
(powdered cellulose)
A naturally occurring substance obtained by chemical preparation and used to add bulk and texture to foods. Found in low-calorie biscuits and cakes, and simulated fruit for pie fillings and so on.

E461 Methylcellulose
Derived from wood pulp by chemical treatment and used as an emulsifier and stabilizer and to add bulk to foods. Found in potato waffles.

E466 Carboxymethylcellulose, sodium salt (CMC)
Made by chemical preparation of cellulose and used to improve the texture and stabilize the moisture of foods. Found in frozen mousses and meringues.

551 Silicon dioxide (Silica)
The main component of sand, it is intensely processed and used as anti-caking agent and thickener and most commonly found in crisps.

621 Sodium hydroden L-glutamate (monoSodium glutamate)
One source of this is sugar beet pulp. It acts as a flavour enhancer by stimulating the secretion of saliva. It is widely used in Chinese foods (see page 13), but it is also found in sausages, pork pies and chilli sauce.

925 Chlorine
Prepared synthetically and used to bleach white flour.

Fresh Foods

The obvious way to cut down your intake of additives is to eat more fresh, natural foods which have not been processed or pre-cooked. However, merely avoiding prepared foods is not a complete guarantee of healthy eating. What is needed is a balanced and varied intake of those foods which supply the nutrients we need to keep us fit and healthy. Your diet should be low in fat and sugar; high in proteins, minerals, vitamins and dietary fibre.

Essential Nutrients

Carbohydrates are needed for energy. Sugar provides short bursts of energy while starch (for example in cereals) provides longer-lasting supplies.

Fats are used by the body to protect and keep it warm and are a concentrated source of energy.

Proteins are necessary for growth and for the development of bones, muscles, skin and blood and for the replacement and repair of tissues and cells.

Minerals are essential to the body, but most are required only in minute quantities. Calcium, iron, iodine and sodium (salt) are the most important.

Vitamins A, B group, C and D are all vital to the body and need to be supplied regularly as they cannot be stored.

Valuable foods

The following are some of the fresh foods which should form the basis of your diet. We also give a brief summary of the valuable nutrients they contain.

These fresh foods are all excellent sources of protein – essential in a healthy diet.

Meat and offal

These are concentrated sources of protein and a variety of vitamins and minerals. Meat does, however, contain a large proportion of fat so select those cuts which have little visible fat.

Pork, ham and bacon are particularly rich in thiamin (vitamin B_1).

Liver is a particularly valuable food in the diet: 100 g (4 oz) calf's (veal) liver yields 45 per cent of the recommended daily intake of protein – as well as enough iron, vitamin A and ribovlavin (vitamin B_2), for two days. It also contains vitamins C and D. Tongue, sweetbreads and tripe are other excellent sources of protein and are all easily digested; tripe also provides calcium. Heart and kidneys are again prime sources of protein and B group vitamins; kidneys are also a rich source of iron.

All offal (variety meat) is relatively fat-free and thus plays an important part in low-fat diets.

Fish

Fish is rich in animal protein, sodium, iodine and nicotinic acid. It is therefore a highly nutritious protein food that is more easily digested than meat.

Oily fish, such as herring and mackerel, are very popular and useful in the diet, providing a valuable source of protein, unsaturated fat, calcium, iron, vitamin D and B group vitamins – riboflavin and nicotinic acid. Oil, containing vitamins A and D, is distributed throughout the flesh of these fish while most other varieties of fish only have oil in the liver which is not normally eaten. Cod and halibut liver oil are thus concentrated sources of the oil-soluble vitamins A and D, and are sometimes used as dietary supplements. Canned salmon and sardines are rich sources of protein and vitamin B group; if the bones are eaten too, they are excellent sources of calcium and phosphorus. However, they are usually canned in either oil or brine and so should be drained well before use.

Shellfish — such as crabs, lobsters, prawns and shrimps — also provide protein, fat and iodine. Molluscs such as oysters, mussels and scallops, are not of such great food value, though they are useful sources of vitamins and minerals.

Milk
Milk is sometimes called the perfect food. It provides sufficient quantities of most of the essential nutrients in an easily digestible form. It is therefore particularly valuable for babies, small children and invalids, but it is an excellent food for everybody. Milk does, however, lack iron, and is deficient in vitamin C, so these nutrients must be supplied by other sources. Natural yogurt is also a valuable food because it contains all the nutrients of milk but is usually made from skimmed milk. It can be used as an ingredient in sweet and savoury dishes, or eaten alone or with natural flavourings (see page 37).

Cheese
While retaining the valuable constituents of milk, cheese is also a valuable source of protein, fat, calcium, vitamin A and riboflavin. Hard cheeses (Cheddar, Gruyère, etc.) are composed of about one-third protein, one-third fat and one-third water. Because of the high fat content, some people find cheese hard to digest but grated cheese is more easily digested and can be combined with a variety of other foods — in salads or cooked dishes.

Eggs
Whole eggs are rich in protein and egg yolk contains plenty of iron; eggs are also useful sources of vitamins A, D and

the B group vitamins. However, they are also a concentrated source of fat and cholesterol, and should be eaten in moderation by those on a low-cholesterol or low-fat diet.

Vegetables
These play an important part in the diet. Besides adding variety and colour to meals, they provide valuable fibre, minerals and vitamins A and C. They also contain protein and starch.

The nutritional content of vegetables varies considerably. As a rough guide, the green leafy vegetables are high in vitamin C – especially broccoli, kale, Brussels sprout, peppers, cabbage, cauliflower, spinach and watercress. These vegetables also provide vitamin A in the form of carotene, some B group vitamins, iron, calcium and other minerals. Root vegetables, especially carrots, are very rich in carotene. Potatoes are, of course, high in starch; although not particularly high in vitamin C, they provide an important source for those who consume large quantities. Potatoes also yield useful amounts of protein, iron and some B group vitamins. Pulses (legumes) are a rich source of vegetable protein, energy and other nutrients and are particularly valuable in a vegetarian diet. Since dried pulses can be stored for long periods they are an essential store cupboard ingredient (see page 28).

Vegetables should be eaten when they are fresh, cooked as little as possible and served raw as often as possible. This is because their nutrients, especially vitamin C and the water soluble B vitamins are sometimes lost during storage, preservation, preparation and cooking.

Fruit
Fruit is a good source of vitamin C and provides us with valuable dietary fibre; some fruits also contain vitamin A. Rosehips, blackcurrant, redcurrants, strawberries and kiwifruit are very rich in vitamin C; oranges, lemons, grapefruit, raspberries, gooseberries and loganberries are good sources; bananas, melons and tangerines only provide a little, while apples, pears and plums are pour sources. Vitamin C is easily lost in cooking, so eat fruit raw whenever possible. Vitamin A is found in small quantities in apricots, tomatoes and peaches.

Storecupboard Ingredients

When trying to cut down on commercially produced foods, because they contain the additives you would prefer to avoid, it is essential to have a storecupboard, well-stocked with basic ingredients. This way, the raw materials you need to make your own pastry, for example, will always be on hand, and you will feel less inclined to reach for the packet mix or ready-made brands.

The other secret of creating your own tasty and appetizing meals from pure foods, rather than opening a can or snipping the top off a packet, is to have a good stock of natural flavourings and to know how to use them to good effect. There are many herbs and spices which we often overlook out of ignorance. A little experimentation, however, will lead you to discover delicious combinations and a vast and unexpected range of flavours.

Cereals

Cereals are a rich source of carbohydrate and therefore provide the body with energy but they also contain small amounts of useful vegetable protein and B group vitamins. The main dietary cereals are wheat, maize (corn), barley, oats, rice and rye. They store well, are relatively cheap to buy, and can be combined with many other ingredients to give a variety of quick and easy meals.

As cereals are mainly carbohydrates, they are more beneficial when eaten with a protein food. For example, breakfast cereal with milk provides a good balance of carbohydrates and protein. Furthermore, the protein value of the cereal is greater than if it were eaten on its own because milk supplies the amino acids which are deficient in cereal. Fresh or dried fruit add valuable vitamins.

Pulses, nuts and dried fruit are valuable foodstuffs that keep well and can be stored for several months.

Dried Fruits

These are a rich source of energy and add flavour to both sweet and savoury dishes. Although the dehydration process destroys practically all vitamin C, most dried fruits are useful sources of other vitamins and minerals. Prunes and dried apricots, for example, are useful sources of carotene; dried figs supply protein and B group vitamins, as well as fibre and energy.

Nuts

Nuts are highly nutritious. They are a rich source of vegetable protein and energy in the form of oil, and contain useful amounts of B group vitamins, iron and calcium.

Pulses

The dried seeds of leguminous plants are known as pulses. They include red, green and brown lentils, chick peas, haricot (navy) beans and so on (see page 29). They are all valuable ingredients because they are particularly rich in protein and provide more energy and B vitamins than either green or root vegetables. Serving pulses with rice or bread is particularly nutritious, since this combination enables the body to derive maximum benefit from the protein these foods contain. For this reason, the popular snack beans on toast is actually very good for you.

Along with wholegrain products and some fruit and vegetables, pulses are an excellent source of dietary fibre. This is the fibrous part of plants that cannot be digested by the body. As it passes through the digestive tract it absorbs moisture, increasing the volume and softness of the food and speeding up its passage through the intestines.

Another function of dietary fibre is to slow down the absorption of sugar into the blood stream, giving a steadier blood sugar level. It is also thought to help control the level of cholesterol in the blood.

Below is a list of the basic ingredients we recommend that you keep in your storecupboard. Some are manufactured products and in these cases you should select those varieties that do not contain food additives. Check all labels carefully before buying.

The basic foods to keep in your storecupboard:

Cereals	**Dried Fruit**
Arrowroot	Apples
Barley	Apricots
Bran	Currants
Brown Rice	Dates
Cornflour (cornstarch)	Desiccated coconut
Couscous	Figs
Cracked wheat	Peaches
Oatmeal	Pears
Oats	Pineapple
Pearl Barley	Prunes
Potato flour	Raisins
Rice flour	Sultanas
Semolina	
Soya flour	**Dried Herbs**
Tapioca	Basil
Wheatgerm	Bay leaves
Wholewheat flour	Bouquet garni
Wholewheat pasta	Caraway seeds

Chevril
Dill
Fennel
Marjoram
Mint
Oregano
Parsley
Rosemary
Sage
Tarragon
Thyme

Drinks and Liquids
Cider
Cocoa powder
Fruit juices, fresh and
    vacuum-sealed packs
    for long-life
Sherry
Wine

Fats and Oils
Corn oil
Butter
Olive oil

Flavourings
Black and white
    peppercorns
Capers
Garlic
Mustard
Salt
Tomato purée (paste)
Vanilla pods or
    essence
Vinegar
Yeast extract

Nuts and Kernels
Chopped, flaked and
    whole nuts

Pulses
Broad beans
Butter beans
Chick peas
Haricot (navy) beans
Kidney beans
Lentils
Split green peas

Spices
Cayenne
Cinnamon
Cloves
Coriander
Cumin
Curry powder
Ginger, root or ground
Mace
Nutmeg
Paprika
Turmeric

Sugars, sweeteners and spreads
Demerara sugar
Granulated sugar
Honey
Icing sugar
Jam
Malt extract
Molasses
Peanut butter
Soft brown sugar
Syrup

Miscellaneous
Baking powder
Bicarbonate of soda
Cream of tartar
Crispbreads
Dried yeast
Gelatine

Breakfasts

It is often tempting to start a busy day with a bowl of commercially produced cereal, milk and sugar. But this is not necessarily the best for your health. Many manufacturers are acknowledging public concern and producing cereals free of salt and sugar, but not all those packages are additive-free. Check the labels, and if you do choose cereals, give them a nutritional lift by adding fresh or dried fruits. Alternatively, try something completely different, like a dried fruit salad or a fruit bread.

FRUIT

Everyone knows that fresh fruit is good for you, but dried fruit is also nutritious and very versatile. Try the recipe on page 32 as an alternative to tinned fruit.

Dried Fruit Compote

Metric/Imperial	*American*
125 g/4 oz dried apple rings	2/3 cup dried apple rings
125 g/4 oz dried prunes	2/3 cup dried prunes
125 g/4 oz dried apricots	2/3 cup dried apricots
50 g/2 oz seedless raisins	1/3 cup seedless raisins
50 g/2 oz figs	1/3 cup figs
grated rind and juice of 1 orange	grated rind and juice of 1 orange
600 ml/1 pint water	2 1/2 cups water
25 g/1 oz blanched almonds	1/4 cup blanched almonds
25 g/1 oz walnut pieces	1/4 cup walnut pieces

Put all the ingredients except the nuts into a large bowl, cover and soak overnight or for 8 to 12 hours.

Next day, put the soaked fruit and any liquid which has not been absorbed into a saucepan and bring to the boil. Cover, reduce heat and simmer very gently for 15 minutes.

Transfer the fruit to a serving dish, mix in the nuts and cool before serving. This salad will keep for several days covered and stored in the refrigerator. Serves 4.

Variation

Chopped and combined with apple purée, this makes a delicious pancake filling.

Compote of Prunes

Metric/Imperial	American
300 ml/½ pint water	1¼ cups water
1 tablespoon molasses	1 tablespoon molasses
500 g/1 lb prunes	2½ cups prunes
¼ cinnamon stick	¼ cinnamon stick
grated rind of ½ lemon	grated rind of ½ lemon

Put the water and molasses into a large bowl, add the prunes and allow to soak overnight. (The water should just cover the prunes.)

Next day, transfer the contents of the bowl to a saucepan with the cinnamon and lemon rind. Add a little more water if necessary to bring the level of the syrup to just below the prunes. Bring to the boil, reduce heat and simmer gently for 30 minutes. Spoon into a serving dish, cool and serve. Serves 4.

Dried Fruit Compote

Heavy Poaching Syrup

(for apples, plums and rhubarb)

Metric/Imperial
500 g/1 lb ripe fresh fruit
6 tablespoons cold water
1 teaspoon lemon juice
125 g/4 oz sugar or 4
   tablespoons honey
1 teaspoon arrowroot
   (optional)

American
1 lb ripe fresh fruit
6 tablespoons cold water
1 teaspoon lemon juice
½ cup sugar or 4
   tablespoons honey
1 teaspoon arrowroot
   (optional)

Prepare the fruit: peel and core apples and cut into quarters; wash and stone plums (removing any discoloration); wash rhubarb, remove any tough or discoloured parts and cut into 5 cm (2 inch) lengths.

Place the water, lemon juice, sugar or honey in a wide shallow pan, cover and heat gently to dissolve the sugar. When all the sugar has dissolved, increase the heat and bring the syrup to the boil.

Add the prepared fruit and immediately lower the heat to a simmer. If poaching apples, baste well to prevent discoloration. Replace the lid and poach for about 20 minutes, testing fruit frequently with a fine skewer or sharp knife. The fruit should be soft, whole, and of a uniform colour.

Transfer the fruit to a serving dish using a slotted spoon. Pour the syrup over the fruit. If desired, the syrup may be thickened. To do this, return it to the boil and add 1 teaspoon arrowroot blended to a paste with a little cold water. Stir constantly. When the syrup clears, pour it over the fruit, cool and serve. Serves 4.

Variations

Apples Add a cinnamon stick to the syrup for extra flavour and serve with Oat Flapjacks (see page 77).

Plums If the syrup is not sweet enough for your taste add a little clear honey while still hot.

Cherries, apricots and greengages To make a Light Poaching syrup for these fruits, use 150 ml/¼ pint (⅔ cup) water and 2 tablespoons clear honey or sugar for every 500 g/1 lb ripe fruit. Make as for Heavy Poaching Syrup.

Oven poaching All the fruits mentioned here can be poached in the oven. The quantities of ingredients for the chosen Syrup are the same but the method is simpler. Place the sugar or honey in an ovenproof dish (preferably one made of heat-resistant glass) and pour over the required amount of lemon juice and boiling water. Stir and add the prepared fruit. Baste well. Cover tightly and bake in a preheated moderate oven (180°C/350°F, Gas Mark 4) for 30 to 40 minutes. Test the fruit frequently towards the end of the cooking time so that it does not become overcooked.

Orange and Banana Starter

Metric/Imperial	*American*
4 oranges, peeled	4 oranges, peeled
1 tablespoon sugar or clear honey	1 tablespoon sugar or honey
3 bananas	3 bananas

Remove the pith from the oranges, using a sharp knife. Segment the fruit, working over a bowl to catch the juices. Place the orange segments in the bowl, stir in the honey or sugar and finally add the sliced bananas. Stir well to prevent the bananas from discolouring. Serves 4.

Strawberry Smoothie

Metric/Imperial	*American*
250 g/8 oz strawberries, hulled	1½ cups strawberries, hulled
1 teaspoon clear honey (optional)	1 teaspoon honey (optional)
4 bananas	4 bananas
1 tablespoon flaked almonds	1 tablespoon slivered almonds

Purée the strawberries and honey together in a blender, or place in a bowl and mash with a fork. Transfer the mixture from the blender to a bowl and chill if desired. Slice the bananas into individual dishes and pour over the purée. Scatter over the almonds and serve immediately. Serves 4.

BREAKFAST BAKES

Commercially produced loaves are often unpackaged, making it impossible to check which chemical additives you are consuming. The simple answer is to make your own. Using the following recipes, move away from the old morning standby, toast, and make breakfast time more imaginative with scones and fruit breads.

Tea Bread

Metric/Imperial
250 g/8 oz mixed dried fruit, chopped
4 oz sugar
150 ml/¼ pint cold tea, strained
1 egg, beaten
1 tablespoon ginger or orange marmalade
250 g/8 oz wholewheat self-raising flour

American
1⅓ cups mixed dried fruit, chopped
½ cup sugar
⅔ cup cold tea, strained
1 egg, beaten
1 tablespoon ginger or orange marmalade
2 cups wholewheat self-rising flour

Place the dried fruit in a large bowl with the sugar. Pour over the strained cold tea and leave to stand overnight.

Next day stir in the egg, marmalade and flour and mix well. Spoon into a buttered 1 kg/2 lb loaf tin (pan). Bake in a preheated moderate oven (160°C/325°F, Gas Mark 3) for 1½ hours, or until firm.

Leave to cool in the tin (pan) for 5 to 10 minutes before turning out on to a wire rack. Allow 2 to 3 days for maturing before cutting. Makes one 1 kg/2 lb loaf.

Bran Teabread

Metric/Imperial
125 g/4 oz bran
125 g/4 oz soft brown sugar
225 g/8 oz mixed dried fruit
300 ml/½ pint milk
125 g/4 oz wholewheat self-raising flour

American
1 cup bran
¾ cup soft brown sugar
1⅓ cups mixed dried fruit
1¼ cups milk
1 cup wholewheat self-rising flour

Mix together the bran, sugar and fruit in a bowl. Stir in the milk and stand for 1 hour. Stir in the sieved flour and transfer the mixture to a greased 450g/1 lb loaf tin (pan). Cook in a preheated moderate oven (180°C/350°F, Gas Mark 4) for 1½ to 2 hours or until cooked. Allow to cool before turning out and serve sliced, with butter. Makes one 450g/1 lb loaf.

Wholewheat Scones

Wholewheat Scones

Metric/Imperial	American
250g/8oz wholewheat self-raising flour	2 cups wholewheat self-rising flour
2 teaspoons baking powder	2 teaspoons baking powder
25g/1oz sugar	2 tablespoons sugar
50g/2oz butter	¼ cup butter
300ml/½ pint milk	1¼ cups milk

Sift all the dry ingredients into a large mixing bowl. Rub (cut) in the butter or margarine until the mixture resembles fine breadcrumbs. Make a well in the centre, pour in the milk, all at once, and mix swiftly to a dough with a palette knife (spatula). Turn out on to a lightly floured surface and knead lightly until the dough is free from cracks.

Roll out the dough to 2cm (¾ inch) thick and using a plain metal cutter, cut out circles 5cm (2 inches) in diameter. Place on lightly greased baking sheets and bake in a preheated hot oven (230°C/450°F, Gas Mark 8) for 12 to 15 minutes until golden brown. Cool on a wire tray, serve with butter and preserves. Makes 8 to 10 scones.

Malt Bread

Metric/Imperial	American
500 g/1 lb wholewheat self-raising flour	4 cups wholewheat self-rising flour
2 teaspoons bicarbonate of soda	2 teaspoons baking soda
300 ml/½ pint milk	1¼ cups milk
2 eggs, beaten	2 eggs, beaten
4 tablespoons golden syrup	4 tablespoons light corn syrup
4 tablespoons malt extract	4 tablespoons malt extract
175 g/6 oz sultanas	1 cup golden raisins

Sift the flour and soda into a large mixing bowl. Combine the milk and eggs and add to the flour, stirring to mix thoroughly.

In a saucepan, melt the syrup with the malt extract, allow to cool slightly, then add this mixture to the bowl, together with the sultanas (golden raisins).

Pour into a 1 kg/2 lb loaf tin (pan). Bake in a preheated moderate oven (180°C/350°F, Gas Mark 4) for 1½ hours. Leave to cool in the tin (pan) for 5 minutes before turning out on to a wire rack. Makes one 1 kg/2 lb loaf.

Orange Bread

Metric/Imperial	American
250 g/8 oz wholewheat self-raising flour or 250 g/8 oz wholewheat plain flour plus 2 teaspoons baking powder	2 cups wholewheat self-rising flour or 2 cups wholewheat all-purpose flour plus 2 teaspoons baking powder
125 g/4 oz sugar	½ cup sugar
grated rind and juice of 2 oranges	grated rind and juice of 2 oranges
1 egg	1 egg
225 ml/7½ fl oz orange juice	⅞ cup orange juice
50 g/2 oz butter, melted	¼ cup butter, melted

Sift the flour and baking powder (if used) into a large mixing bowl. Add the sugar and grated orange rind and mix well. Beat the egg, add the orange juice and melted butter and stir into the flour to make a smooth, soft batter. Pour into a greased and lined 1 kg/2 lb loaf tin (pan).

Bake in a preheated moderate oven (180°C/350°F, Gas Mark 4) for about 50 minutes, until firm or until a skewer inserted in the centre comes out clean. Allow to cool for 5 to 10 minutes before turning out on to a wire rack. Serve cold with butter or preserves. Makes one 1 kg/2 lb loaf.

Granola

Metric/Imperial	American
250 g/8 oz rolled oats	2¼ cups rolled oats
50 g/2 oz sesame seeds	⅓ cup sesame seeds
50 g/2 oz sunflower seeds	⅓ cup sunflower seeds
50 g/2 oz pumpkin seeds	⅓ cup pumpkin seeds
125 g/4 oz shredded fresh or desiccated coconut	1⅓ cups shredded coconut
50 g/2 oz chopped pecan nuts	½ cup chopped pecan nuts
50 g/2 oz raisins	⅓ cup raisins
grated rind of 1 orange	grated rind of 1 orange

Spread the oats out in a grill (broiler) pan and toast under moderate heat for a few minutes until crisp and slightly brown. Cool and then mix all the ingredients together in a large bowl. Store in an airtight container.

Serve with milk and a little honey if liked, or a spoonful of yogurt. Makes 750 g/1½ lb granola. Approximately 2 tablespoons per portion is normally sufficient.

Yogurt

Yogurt is an excellent source of protein and calcium and makes a pleasant and refreshing change in the mornings from cereal and toast. Avoid yogurts which contain additives and artificial flavourings and opt instead for natural yogurt to which you can add your own flavourings. Here are some suggestions:

Fruit Stir in 2 tablespoons of any puréed fruit per portion.
Nuts Sprinkle over chopped mixed nuts.
Honey Swirl a teaspoon of runny honey into each portion.

Starters

Starters, like all curtain-raisers, should stimulate the appetite but not overwhelm it. This mini-course also provides the perfect opportunity to redress the balance of your meal. If the main course is creamy, choose a crisp starter; if cooked vegetables accompany the main attraction, start with a salad.

Marinated Mushrooms

Marinated Mushrooms

Metric/Imperial
350 g/12 oz button
   mushrooms
2 tablespoons vinegar
2 tablespoons oil
1 teaspoon lemon juice
½ teaspoon dried basil
½ teaspoon dried
   marjoram
½ teaspoon mustard seed
2 tablespoons finely diced
   onion (optional)
1 tablespoon freshly
   chopped parsley

American
3 cups button mushrooms
2 tablespoons vinegar
2 tablespoons oil
1 teaspoon lemon juice
½ teaspoon dried basil
½ teaspoon dried
   marjoram
½ teaspoon mustard seed
2 tablespoons finely diced
   onion (optional)
1 tablespoon freshly
   chopped parsley

Wipe the mushrooms and cut off any unsightly stalks (stems).

Combine all the remaining ingredients (except the chives) and pour over the mushrooms, stir to mix well and cover with plastic wrap. Set aside to marinate for 24 hours.

To serve, stir in the parsley or chives, adjust the seasoning and spoon on to individual dishes. Serve with hot wholewheat garlic bread or rolls. Serves 6.

Cottage Cheese and Date Starter

Metric/Imperial	*American*
2 oranges	2 oranges
4 sticks celery, thinly sliced	4 stalks celery, thinly sliced
1 tablespoon snipped chives	1 tablespoon snipped chives
salt	salt
freshly ground pepper	freshly ground pepper
125 g/4 oz fresh dates, halved and stoned	¼ lb fresh dates, halved and pitted
2 tablespoons vinaigrette (see page 64)	2 tablespoons vinaigrette (see page 64)
225 g/8 oz cottage cheese	1 cup cottage cheese
2 heads chicory	2 heads endive
1 tablespoon lemon juice	1 tablespoon lemon juice
50 g/2 oz peanuts, chopped	⅓ cup chopped peanuts
1 bunch watercress to garnish	1 bunch watercress to garnish

Peel the oranges (reserving the skin) and, with a sharp knife, cut away all the white pith. Carefully ease out the segments from between the membranes. Place in a mixing bowl and add the celery, chives, salt and pepper and the dates.

Finely grate some of the orange rind and add 1 tablespoon to the vinaigrette. Pour over the salad and toss lightly. Carefully fold in the cottage cheese.

Arrange the chicory leaves on 4 small plates and sprinkle with lemon juice. Spoon the cottage cheese mixture into the centre of each plate and sprinkle with chopped nuts. Garnish with watercress and serve immediately. Serves 4.

Cucumber Stuffed Tomatoes

Metric/Imperial	*American*
12 medium tomatoes	12 medium tomatoes
1 medium cucumber, seeded and sliced	1 medium cucumber, seeded and sliced
½ onion, finely chopped	½ onion, finely chopped
150 g/5 oz plain yogurt	⅔ cup plain yogurt
1-2 tablespoons finely chopped mint	1-2 tablespoons finely chopped mint
salt	salt
freshly ground pepper	freshly ground pepper
chinese lettuce leaves to garnish	stem lettuce to garnish
pumpernickel to serve	pumpernickel to serve

Cut a generous slice from the top of each tomato to form a lid. Scoop out the seeds, pulp and core, and turn the tomato shells upside down to drain.

Combine the remaining filling ingredients in a bowl, seasoning to taste, and stir well. Spoon into tomato shells, replace lids and serve chilled on a bed of Chinese leaves (stem lettuce), with pumpernickel. Serves 6.

Brown Rice Stuffed Tomatoes

Metric/Imperial	*American*
12 medium tomatoes	12 medium tomatoes
250 g/8 oz cooked brown rice	1⅓ cups cooked brown rice
3 tablespoons raisins	3 tablespoons raisins
1 small green pepper, cored, seeded and diced	1 small green pepper, seeded and diced
1 small red pepper, cored, seeded and diced	1 small red pepper, seeded and diced
Dressing:	*Dressing:*
4 tablespoons olive oil	4 tablespoons olive oil
3 tablespoons lemon juice	3 tablespoons lemon juice
1 tablespoon mango chutney	1 tablespoon mango chutney
½ teaspoon curry powder	½ teaspoon curry powder
watercress, to garnish	watercress, for garnish

Prepare the tomatoes as in the previous recipe. Set aside until the stuffing is ready.

Combine the rice, raisins and peppers in a bowl. Mix all the dressing ingredients in a screw-top jar and shake well. Pour the dressing over the rice, toss and adjust the seasoning. Spoon into tomato shells, replace lids and serve chilled, garnished with watercress. Serves 6.

Avocados with Shellfish

Metric/Imperial	American
2 ripe avocados	2 ripe avocados
1 tablespoon lemon juice	1 tablespoon lemon juice
1 medium tomato, skinned, seeded and chopped	1 medium tomato, skinned, seeded and chopped
250 g/8 oz cooked peeled prawns	½ lb cooked shelled shrimp
2 spring onions, finely chopped	2 scallions, finely chopped
Dressing:	*Dressing:*
salt	salt
freshly ground pepper	freshly ground pepper
½ tablespoon cider vinegar	½ tablespoon cider vinegar
½ tablespoon water	½ tablespoon water
2 tablespoons corn or sunflower oil	2 tablespoons corn or sunflower oil
watercress sprigs and lemon wedges to garnish	watercress sprigs and lemon wedges for garnish

Cut each avocado in half, remove the stone and carefully scoop out the flesh with a tablespoon, taking care to keep the shell intact.

Brush the inside of each shell with some of the lemon juice to prevent discoloration and set aside.

Dice the avocado pulp and combine with the tomato in a bowl. Mix all the dressing ingredients together, pour over the avocado mixture, add the prawns (shrimp) and mix gently.

Pile the mixture into the reserved shells, cover closely with plastic wrap and chill. Serve as soon as possible after making and garnish with watercress sprigs and lemon wedges. Serves 4.

Stocks and Soups

Packet soups, canned soups and the good old stock cube are all familiar props in the kitchen – but they are not as healthful as we are led to believe. Nearly all canned soups contain high levels of salt and many contain sugar; packet soups and stock cubes contain artificial flavourings and additives.

Home-made stocks and soups, on the other hand, have a far better flavour and are equally simple and speedy to make – particularly if you use a blender or food processor. An ingenious time-saving tip is to make a concentrated stock and then freeze it in ice cube trays to make handy stock cubes.

Chicken Stock

Metric/Imperial	*American*
1 roast chicken carcass	1 roast chicken carcass
1 whole carrot	1 whole carrot
1 whole onion	1 whole onion
750 ml/1¼ pints water	3 cups water
1 bay leaf	1 bay leaf
pinch of salt	pinch of salt
6 black peppercorns	6 black peppercorns

Break up the chicken carcass and place in a large saucepan with all the remaining ingredients.

Bring to the boil and skim off any surface scum. Reduce the heat and simmer for 1-1½ hours, topping up the water level if it drops below that of the bones. Strain the stock.

Remove all traces of fat from the stock and store in the refrigerator until required. Makes about 750 ml/1¼ pints (3 cups).

Vegetable Stock

Metric/Imperial	*American*
1 onion, sliced	1 onion, sliced
1 stick celery, chopped	1 stalk celery, chopped
1 large carrot, chopped	1 large carrot, chopped
1 medium potato, chopped	1 medium potato, chopped
3 sprigs parsley	3 sprigs parsley
2.5 litres/4 pints water	10 cups water

Place the vegetables, herbs and peppercorns in a large saucepan and add the water. Bring to the boil, then turn the heat down, cover and simmer for 1 hour. Strain through a sieve. Makes 1.2 litres/2 pints (5 cups).

Beef Stock

Metric/Imperial	American
1 kg/2 lb marrow and shin bones	2 lb marrow or shin bones
2.5 litres/4 pints water	10 cups water
salt	salt
1 onion, quartered	1 onion, quartered
2 carrots, chopped	2 carrots, chopped
1 bouquet garni	1 bouquet garni
6 black peppercorns	6 black peppercorns

Put the bones in a large saucepan. Cover with the water and add 2 teaspoons salt. Bring to the boil, skimming off any scum. Half cover with a lid and simmer for 2 hours.

Add the vegetables, bouquet garni and peppercorns and simmer for a further 1½-2 hours, adding more water if the level drops below that of the bones. Strain, leave to cool, then skim off fat with a spoon or absorbent kitchen paper. Use immediately or keep in the refrigerator. Makes 1.25 litres/2 pints (5 cups).

Scotch Broth, page 44

Scotch Broth

Metric/Imperial	American
450 g/1 lb middle neck of lamb, cut into small pieces	1 lb middle neck of lamb, cut into small pieces
2.7 litres/5 pints water	12 cups water
2 onions, finely chopped	2 onions, finely chopped
225 g/8 oz carrots, finely chopped	2 cups finely chopped carrot
2 leeks, thinly sliced	3 cups sliced leek
50 g/2 oz pearl barley	1/3 cup pearl barley
salt	salt
freshly ground pepper	freshly ground pepper
1 tablespoon chopped parsley	1 tablespoon chopped parsley

Place the meat in a large saucepan with the water. Bring to the boil and skim off the fat and skum. Add the barley and simmer for 30 minutes. Add the vegetables and season with salt and pepper. Cover and simmer for 1½ to 2 hours.

Remove the bones from the broth and strip off as much meat as possible. Stir the meat back into the broth and check the seasoning. Sprinkle with parsley. Serves 6.

Mushroom Soup

Metric/Imperial	American
250 g/8 oz mushrooms, diced	2 cups diced mushrooms
1 medium onion, finely chopped	1 medium onion, finely chopped
900 ml/1½ pints Chicken Stock (see page 42)	3¾ cups Chicken Stock (see page 42)
1 bouquet garni	1 bouquet garni
½ teaspoon dried basil	½ teaspoon dried basil
salt	salt
freshly ground pepper	freshly ground pepper
2 tablespoons cornflour or potato flour	2 tablespoons cornstarch or potato flour
wholewheat croûtons to garnish	wholewheat croûtons to garnish

Place the mushrooms and onions in a large saucepan with 150 ml/¼ pint (⅔ cup) stock. Bring to the boil, then simmer for 10 minutes or until tender. Add the remaining stock with the herbs and seasonings and continue to simmer for 20 minutes. Remove the bouquet garni.

To thicken, blend the cornflour (cornstarch) with a little stock or water. Bring the soup to just below boiling point and add the cornflour (cornstarch) stirring constantly until thickened. Adjust the seasoning and serve with croûtons. Serves 3-4.

Leek and Celery Soup

Metric/Imperial	American
25 g/1 oz butter	2 tablespoons butter
1 medium leek, roughly chopped	1 cup chopped leek
1 small head celery, roughly chopped	1 small bunch celery, roughly chopped
1 medium onion, chopped	1 medium onion, chopped
300 ml/½ pint Chicken Stock (page 42)	1¼ cups Chicken Stock (page 42)
salt	salt
freshly ground pepper	freshly ground pepper
1 blade of mace	1 blade of mace
300 ml/½ pint milk	1¼ cups milk
25 g/1 oz cornflour or potato flour	¼ cup cornstarch or potato flour
1 tablespoon chopped parsley to garnish	1 tablespoon chopped parsley to garnish

Melt the butter in a large saucepan and add the vegetables. Stir them, cover and cook gently for 5 minutes until soft and lightly coloured. Add the stock, seasonings and mace and bring to the boil. Reduce heat, cover and simmer gently for 20 minutes. Remove the mace.

Purée the soup in a blender or by pressing through a sieve. Return to the rinsed pan and reheat with the milk. To thicken, blend the cornflour (cornstarch) with a little cold stock or water and add to the soup, stirring constantly. Adjust the seasoning and serve very hot, topped with chopped parsley. Serves 3-4.

Vegetables and Salads

More and more people are serving vegetables as the main ingredient of the meal. Carefully cooked and beautifully presented, they can steal the limelight from many a meat-based main course, but soggy overcooked offerings contribute nothing either nutritionally or in terms of appearance.

To get the most from your vegetables buy only fresh and crisp vegetables and prepare them just before cooking. (Frozen vegetables are handy and do not normally contain additives, but check the packet.) Never overcook and never add bicarbonate of soda to the cooking water as this destroys the vitamin C.

Cabbage in White Sauce

Metric/Imperial	American
1 spring cabbage, shredded	1 spring cabbage, shredded
salt	salt
freshly ground pepper	freshly ground pepper
½ onion, grated	½ onion, grated
Sauce:	*Sauce:*
300 ml/½ pint milk	1¼ cups milk
1 tablespoon cornflour	1 tablespoon cornstarch
salt	salt
freshly ground pepper	freshly ground pepper
pinch of freshly grated nutmeg	pinch of freshly ground nutmeg

Place the shredded cabbage in a saucepan with enough boiling water to cover. Season to taste with salt and pepper, add the onion and cook for 10 to 15 minutes over moderate heat until just tender.

Meanwhile prepare the sauce. Heat most of the milk until almost boiling. In another pan, mix the cornflour (cornstarch) to a paste with the remaining milk and pour on the hot milk. Return the pan to the heat and bring the sauce to the boil, stirring constantly until thick and smooth. Stir in the salt and pepper and nutmeg.

When the cabbage is cooked, drain it thoroughly and return to the heat to dry off excess moisture. Transfer to a hot serving dish, add the sauce, and fold lightly together with a metal spoon. Serves 4-6.

Ratatouille

Ratatouille

Metric/Imperial	American
4 courgettes, sliced	4 zucchini, sliced
4 tomatoes, skinned and quartered	4 tomatoes, skinned and quartered
2 medium aubergines, sliced	2 medium aubergines, sliced
2 onions, sliced	2 onions, sliced
2 large red peppers, cored, seeded and sliced	2 large red peppers, cored, seeded and sliced
2 bay leaves	2 bay leaves
300 ml/½ pint tomato juice	1¼ cups tomato juice
salt	salt
freshly ground pepper	freshly ground pepper

Place all the vegetables in a saucepan with the bay leaves, tomato juice, salt and pepper. Bring to the boil and skim. Cover and simmer for about 20 minutes or until all the vegetables are tender. If there is too much tomato juice, reduce by boiling briskly for a few minutes. Spoon on to individual dishes and serve as a side dish. Serves 4-6.

Celery Crunch

Metric/Imperial	*American*
25 g/1 oz butter	2 tablespoons butter
50-75 g/2-3 oz brazil nuts, roughly chopped	¾ cup brazil nuts, roughly chopped
2 tablespoons oil	2 tablespoons oil
1 small head celery, cut in matchstick strips	1 small head celery, cut in matchstick strips
½ green pepper, seeded and cut in matchstick strips	½ green pepper, seeded and cut in matchstick strips
½ red pepper, seeded and cut in matchstick strips	½ red pepper, seeded and cut in matchstick strips
salt	salt
freshly ground pepper	freshly ground pepper

Melt the butter in a small saucepan, add the nuts and sauté until golden. Set aside.

Heat a large wok or frying pan (skillet) for 1 minute, add the oil and heat for a further minute. Add the celery and peppers and sauté, stirring and turning for about 1½ minutes. Add the buttered brazils and sauté for about 30 seconds or until all the ingredients are very hot. Season with salt and pepper and serve immediately. Serves 4.

Stir-Fried Broccoli

Metric/Imperial	*American*
750 g/1½ lb broccoli	1½ lb broccoli
2 tablespoons oil	2 tablespoons oil
salt	salt
freshly ground pepper	freshly ground pepper

Wash the broccoli thoroughly. Separate into sprigs and cut the stalks into strips. Keep stalks and sprigs apart.

Heat a large wok or frying pan (skillet) for about 1 minute, add the oil and heat for 1 minute more until very hot. Add the broccoli stalks, stirring and turning constantly for 1 minute. Add the sprigs and sauté, stirring and turning, for 1 minute more. The broccoli should still be crisp but thoroughly heated and of good colour.

Remove from the heat, season with salt and pepper and serve immediately. Serves 4.

Variations

A little powdered ginger (to taste) may be stirred in just before serving.

For a contrast in colour and texture, serve with cooked chick peas. Heat the chick peas in a separate pan and surround the broccoli with them.

3 to 4 tablespoons small garlic croûtons (see below) make a delicious garnish.

Garlic Croûtons

Peel and slice a garlic clove and gently sauté in oil. Remove the slices and discard. Cut slices of bread into cubes and fry in the oil until golden and crisp. Drain on absorbent kitchen paper.

Beetroot in Soured Cream

Metric/Imperial	*American*
butter for frying	butter for frying
4 medium-sized beetroot, cooked and sliced	4 medium-sized beet, cooked and sliced
½ teaspoon ground allspice	½ teaspoon ground allspice
salt	salt
freshly ground pepper	freshly ground pepper
150 ml/¼ pint soured cream, at room temperature	⅔ cup soured cream, at room temperature
snipped chives to garnish	snipped chives to garnish
1 tablespoon chopped almonds	1 tablespoon chopped almonds

Melt a knob of butter in a large heavy-based saucepan. Add the sliced beetroot and sprinkle with the allspice. Season with salt and pepper to taste, and then fry lightly in the oil until hot.

Turn off the heat and stir in the soured cream. Transfer to a hot serving dish and sprinkle with snipped chives and chopped nuts. Serves 4.

Beetroot in Soured Cream, page 60; French Beans with Bacon

French Beans with Bacon

Metric/Imperial	American
450 g/1 lb French beans	1 lb green beans
salt	salt
butter for frying	butter for frying
½ small onion, chopped	½ small onion, chopped
100 g/4 oz streaky bacon, derinded and chopped	½ cup chopped, derinded fatty bacon
freshly ground pepper	freshly ground pepper
To finish:	*To finish:*
4 tablespoons single cream	4 tablespoons light cream
1 tablespoon chopped mint	1 tablespoon chopped mint

Cook the beans in boiling, salted water for 12 to 15 minutes
or until just tender. Drain.

Meanwhile, melt a knob of butter in a frying pan. Add the
onions and bacon and fry until the onions are golden and
the bacon pieces are crisp. Stir in the drained beans and
season to taste with salt and pepper. Heat through, stirring
constantly. Stir in the cream and mint or parsley and
transfer to a hot serving dish. Serve immediately. Serves 4.

Vegetable Medley

Vegetable Medley

Choose at least 4 from the following: carrots, peppers, onions, spinach, white or spring cabbage, cauliflower, broccoli, courgettes (zucchini), young peas, sliced green beans, mange tout (snow peas), mushrooms. Cut into florets and small strips.

Metric/Imperial	American
1 garlic clove	1 garlic clove
2-3 tablespoons corn oil	2-3 tablespoons corn oil
500 g/1 lb mixed vegetables	1 lb mixed vegetables
salt	salt
freshly ground pepper	freshly ground pepper
a pinch of nutmeg	a pinch of nutmeg

Rub the garlic around a large frying pan (skillet) or wok. Heat the pan or wok for 1 minute, add the oil and heat for a further minute. Add the vegetables and sauté, stirring and turning for about 2 minutes until just tender. Remove from the heat, season with salt, pepper and nutmeg and serve immediately. Serves 4.

Brown Rice Pilaff

Metric/Imperial	American
50 g/2 oz butter	¼ cup butter
175 g/6 oz brown rice	1 cup brown rice
50 g/2 oz chopped onion	½ cup chopped onion
1 garlic clove, crushed	1 garlic clove, crushed
750 ml/1¼ pints Chicken or Vegetable Stock (see page 42)	3 cups pints Chicken or Vegetable Stock (see page 42)
salt	salt
freshly ground pepper	freshly ground pepper

Melt the butter in a large saucepan over moderate heat, add the rice and sauté, stirring, for 1 minute.

Add the onion and garlic and sauté for 1 minute more, then pour over the stock and season to taste. Bring to the boil, cover and simmer for 35 to 40 minutes until the stock has been absorbed. Serve immediately. Serves 3.

Variation

For a vegetable pilaff, add 2 tomatoes, peeled and chopped, and 250 g/8 oz chopped mixed vegetables to the rice after it has been cooking for about 25 minutes. Cook for a further 10 to 15 minutes.

Sunshine Salad

Metric/Imperial	American
350 g/12 oz frozen sweetcorn kernels	¾ lb frozen whole kernel corn
1 small red pepper, seeded and diced	1 small red pepper, seeded and diced
1 tablespoon chopped spring onions	1 tablespoon chopped scallions
2 tablespoons roughly chopped walnuts	2 tablespoons roughly chopped walnuts
3 tablespoons vinaigrette (see page 64)	3 tablespoons vinaigrette (see page 64)
3-4 tablespoons mayonnaise (see page 87)	3-4 tablespoons mayonnaise (see page 87)
salt	salt
freshly ground pepper	freshly ground pepper

Cook the corn according to packet instructions, drain and imediately plunge into chilled water to arrest further cooking and retain colour. Spread on absorbent kitchen paper to dry, then transfer to a bowl.

Add the red pepper, spring onions (scallions), chopped walnuts and vinaigrette and mix well. Stir in the mayonnaise and mix thoroughly. Adjust the seasoning, transfer to a salad bowl and chill before serving. Serves 2-4.

Butter Bean Salad

Metric/Imperial	American
175 g/6 oz butter beans, soaked, cooked and drained (see page 54)	6 oz cannellini, soaked, cooked and drained (see page 54)
1 stick celery, finely diced	1 stalk celery, finely diced
1 small red pepper, seeded and diced	1 small red pepper, seeded and diced
1 × 7.5 cm/3 inch length of cucumber, diced	1 × 3 inch length of cucumber, diced
1 onion, finely chopped	1 onion, finely chopped
2 garlic cloves, crushed	2 garlic cloves, crushed
Dressing:	*Dressing:*
1 egg yolk	1 egg yolk
1 teaspoon dry mustard	1 teaspoon dry mustard
salt	salt
freshly ground pepper	freshly ground pepper
6 tablespoons oil	6 tablespoons oil
2 tablespoons red wine vinegar	2 tablespoons red wine vinegar
1 tablespoon lemon juice	1 tablespoon lemon juice

Combine the vegetables in a large salad bowl and toss with half the garlic. Cover with plastic wrap and place in the refrigerator to chill while you prepare the dressing.

Place the egg yolk in a bowl with the mustard, seasoning and remaining garlic. Add the oil drop by drop, whisking well between additions.

When all the oil has been added, whisk in the vinegar and lemon juice to give the sauce the consistency of single (light) cream. Add more vinegar if necessary. Pour over the prepared vegetables, toss and serve. Serves 4.

Pulses and Pasta

Kidney Bean Casserole; Broad Bean and Green Pea Casserole; Butter Bean Bake, page 57

Pulses are dried beans, peas and lentils. Although they need some pre-soaking, with a little forethought they can be incorporated into your cooking as easily as any other vegetable. Moreover they are an excellent source of protein, vitamins and fibre and an invaluable part of your diet.

Approximate Cooking Times

Pulse	Simmering	Pressure Cooking (15 lb pressure)
Butter Beans (Cannellini)	1½ hours	25 minutes
Haricot (Navy) Beans	1 to 1½ hours	25 to 30 minutes
Red Kidney Beans★	1 to 1½ hours	20 to 25 minutes
Chick Peas	2 hours	25 to 30 minutes
Blackeyed Peas	1 hour	15 to 20 minutes
Whole Dried Peas	1 hour	20 minutes
Split Peas	45 minutes	15 minutes
Red Split Lentils (soaked)	15-20 minutes	10 minutes
Red Split Lentils (unsoaked)	20-30 minutes	15 minutes

★ *The first 10 minutes of cooking should be a fast boil to kill harmful toxins.*

Kidney Bean Casserole

Metric/Imperial
450 g/1 lb red kidney
  beans, cooked (see
  page 57)
2 onions, sliced
2 rashers bacon, fat
  removed and chopped
300 ml/½ pint Chicken
  Stock (see page 42)
salt
freshly ground pepper

American
1 lb red kidney beans,
  cooked (see page 57)
2 onions, sliced
2 slices bacon, fat removed
  and chopped
1¼ cups Chicken Stock
  (see page 42)
salt
freshly ground pepper

Place the kidney beans, onions and bacon in a saucepan. Pour over just enough stock to cover and add salt and pepper. Simmer gently for about 10 minutes or until the onions are tender. Turn into a heated serving dish. Serves 4.

Broad Bean and Green Pea Casserole

Metric/Imperial
450 g/1 lb green peas
450 g/1 lb broad beans
salt
1 tablespoon cornflour
300 ml/½ pint milk
300 ml/½ pint stock or
  vegetable cooking liquid
  (see method)
pinch of dried rosemary
freshly ground pepper

American
1 lb green peas
1 lb lima beans
salt
1 tablespoon cornstarch
1¼ cups milk
1¼ cups stock or vegetable
  cooking liquid (see
  method)
pinch of dried rosemary
freshly ground pepper

Place the peas and beans together in a saucepan of boiling salted water and cook for about 15 minutes until tender. Drain, reserving the cooking liquid.

Mix the cornflour (cornstarch) and milk together and heat gently, stirring. Add 300 ml/½ pint vegetable cooking liquid or stock, rosemary and salt and pepper to taste. Add the peas and beans and heat together for about 2 minutes, then turn into a heated serving dish. Serves 4-6.

Butter Bean Bake

Metric/Imperial	*American*
600 ml/1 pint Cheese Sauce (see page 61)	2½ cups Cheese Sauce (see page 61)
300 g/10 oz frozen sweetcorn kernels, cooked and drained	10 oz frozen whole kernel corn, cooked and drained
250 g/8 oz butter beans, soaked, cooked and drained (see page 54)	½ lb cannellini, soaked, cooked and drained (see page 54)
2 tablespoons wheatgerm	2 tablespoons wheatgerm
½ teaspoon caraway seeds	½ teaspoon caraway seeds

Combine the sauce, corn and beans in a large ovenproof dish. Sprinkle over the wheatgerm, cover and place in a preheated moderate oven (180°C/350°F, Gas Mark 4) for 20 to 30 minutes until bubbly.

Remove from the oven, sprinkle over the caraway seeds and serve hot. Serves 4.

PASTA

You can make your own pasta using the recipe here, though the wholewheat pastas produced by many manufacturers are an excellent alternative and contain nothing but wholewheat flour and natural ingredients.

Pauline's Wholewheat Pasta

Metric/Imperial	*American*
250 g/8 oz wholewheat flour	2 cups wholewheat flour
½ teaspoon salt	½ teaspoon salt
120 ml/4 fl oz cold water	½ cup cold water
2½ tablespoons oil	2½ tablespoons oil

Sift the flour and salt into a large bowl. Add most of the water and all the oil. Mix together with your fingers to a dough, then turn on to a lightly floured working surface and knead thoroughly until smooth and no longer sticky.

Turn the bowl upside down over the dough and rest for 15 to 20 minutes. This allows the gluten to soften and makes the dough softer and more elastic.

Roll out the dough as thinly as possible. Cut into rectangles, about 7.5×15 cm/3×6 inches. The dough should produce about 20 sheets.

Pasta Shells in Spicy Tomato Sauce

Metric/Imperial	American
175 g/6 oz wholewheat pasta shells	1½ cups wholewheat pasta shells
½ teaspoon salt	½ teaspoon salt
Sauce:	*Sauce:*
1 tablespoon oil	1 tablespoon oil
1 onion, chopped	1 onion, chopped
1 garlic clove, crushed	1 garlic clove, crushed
1 green pepper, cored, seeded and chopped	1 green pepper, seeded and chopped
125 g/4 oz mushrooms, sliced	1 cup sliced mushrooms
1×450 g/15 oz can chopped tomatoes	1×16 oz can chopped tomatoes
1 teaspoon dried mixed herbs or 2 teaspoons chopped fresh herbs	1 teaspoon dried mixed herbs or 2 teaspoons chopped fresh herbs
1 bay leaf	1 bay leaf
a pinch of chilli powder	a pinch of chili powder
freshly ground pepper	freshly ground pepper
grated Parmesan cheese to serve	grated Parmesan cheese to serve

Cook the pasta in plenty of boiling salted water for 15 to 20 minutes until tender but still firm to the bite.

Meanwhile heat the oil in a large saucepan and gently sauté the onion and garlic for 5 minutes until soft but not coloured. Add the green pepper and mushrooms and cook for 2 minutes. Stir in the tomatoes, with their juice, herbs and seasonings. Cover and cook for about 15 minutes over moderate heat.

When the pasta shells are cooked, drain them well and add to the tomato mixture. Toss, adjust the seasoning, remove the bay leaf and serve piping hot with grated Parmesan. Serves 2-3.

Gnocchi alla Romana

Metric/Imperial	American
600 ml/1 pint milk	2½ cups milk
125 g/4 oz semolina	⅔ cup semolina flour
1 egg yolk	1 egg yolk
40 g/1½ oz butter	3 tablespoons butter
salt	salt
freshly ground pepper	freshly ground pepper
a pinch of grated nutmeg	a pinch of grated nutmeg
50 g/2 oz Cheddar cheese, grated	½ cup shredded Cheddar cheese
300 ml/½ pint hot Economical Tomato Sauce (see page 60)	1¼ cups hot Economical Tomato Sauce (see page 60)
parsley to garnish	parsley to garnish

Bring the milk to the boil in a heavy saucepan. Sprinkle on the semolina, whisking well. When all the semolina has been absorbed, beat the mixture with a wooden spoon over moderate heat for 2 minutes. Reduce the heat and simmer gently until cooked – about 6 to 8 minutes.

Remove from the heat and beat in the egg yolk, 2 tablespoons of the butter, salt, pepper and nutmeg.

Pour on to a lightly oiled baking sheet or Swiss roll tin (jelly roll pan) to a depth of about 5 mm/¼ inch. Level the surface and set aside to cool.

When cold, cut into rounds with a 5 cm/2 inch cutter. Place any scraps in a mound in the centre of a shallow buttered dish. Arrange the cut rounds neatly on the top, making an 'island' in the dish. Melt the remaining butter and brush over the gnocchi.

Sprinkle the cheese over the top. Lightly brown under a preheated hot grill (broiler) for 3 to 4 minutes.

To serve, pour the piping hot tomato sauce into the dish, surrounding the gnocchi, and garnish with parsley or watercress. Serves 4.

Variation
Spinach Gnocchi Cook and finely chop 250 g/8 oz fresh or frozen spinach. Stir this into the semolina mixture before spreading it over the baking sheet.

Sauces

What does the word 'sauce' conjure up for you? A French chef lovingly nursing a *roux*, or a busy housewife snipping the top off a packet mix?

Neither need be the true picture. Many great sauces can be made in moments from pure wholesome ingredients, while the more elaborate can be made in bulk and batched in handy amounts in the freezer, making them just as accessible as the packet or can.

Economical Tomato Sauce, page 60; Mushroom Sauce, page 61

Economical Tomato Sauce

Metric/Imperial	American
75 g/3 oz margarine or butter	6 tablespoons margarine or butter
50 g/2 oz diced carrot	⅓ cup diced carrot
75 g/3 oz plain white flour	¾ cup all-purpose white flour
600 ml/1 pint Chicken or Vegetable Stock (see page 42)	2½ cups Chicken or Vegetable Stock (see page 42)
1 × 425 g/15 oz can tomatoes	1 × 15 oz can tomatoes
1 tablespoon tomato purée	1 tablespoon tomato paste
1 teaspoon sugar	1 teaspoon sugar
1 garlic clove, crushed	1 garlic clove, crushed
1 bay leaf	1 bay leaf
pinch of basil	pinch of basil
salt	salt
freshly ground pepper	freshly ground pepper

Melt the margarine in a large heavy saucepan, add the carrot and onion and sauté gently, covered, for 5 minutes, until the vegetables are soft but not coloured. Stir in the flour and cook for 1 minute. Gradually blend in the stock, stirring constantly. Add the remaining ingredients, mix well, and bring to the boil. Reduce the heat, cover and simmer gently for 30 to 45 minutes, stirring occasionally. Add a little water if necessary.

Strain the sauce into a large clean pan, pressing the ingredients against the sides of the strainer to extract all the liquid. Adjust the seasoning and reheat. Serve hot. Makes about 900 ml/1½ pints (3¾ cups) sauce.

Variation

Barbecue Sauce Make as Economical Tomato Sauce but add 3 chopped sticks (stalks) celery with the carrot and onion. After adding the stock, stir in 2 slices of lemon, 2 tablespoons malt vinegar, 1 tablespoon Worcestershire sauce and 1 bouquet garni with the remaining ingredients as in the tomato sauce recipe. Cook, strain and serve as above. This is delicious served with pork chops or sausages, spare-ribs (country-style pork ribs), grills (broils) or with pulses.

Helpful Hint
To freeze, cool quickly, then pour into suitable containers, seal (leaving 2.5 cm/1 inch headspace) and freeze. Store for up to 3 months. To thaw, place the frozen sauce block in a heavy saucepan with 1 tablespoon water. Heat gently, stirring occasionally, until the sauce is thawed, then increase the heat to just below boiling point.

Basic White Sauce

Metric/Imperial	American
2 tablespoons cornflour	2 tablespoons cornstarch
600 ml/1 pint milk	2½ cups milk
salt	salt
freshly ground pepper	freshly ground pepper

Heat most of the milk until almost boiling. In another pan, mix the cornflour (cornstarch) to a paste with the remaining milk. Pour on the hot milk.

Return to the heat and cook, stirring, until the mixture thickens. Season and continue to cook for 2 to 3 minutes before serving. Makes 600 ml/1 pint (2½ cups).

Variations

Béchamel Purists prefer this to the Basic White Sauce, as it has a deeper flavour. Before preparing the sauce, heat the milk with 1 onion stuck with 4 cloves, 1 bay leaf and a bouquet garni. Bring to just below boiling point, remove from the heat, cover and let stand for 30 minutes. Strain and use as for Basic White Sauce (above).

Cheese To the completed white sauce add 30 g/1 oz (¼ cup) grated cheese, salt, white pepper and a pinch of cayenne pepper, whisking until smooth and creamy.

Parsley To the completed white sauce add 2 tablespoons chopped fresh parsley and salt and white pepper to taste. Whisk until the sauce is smooth. Serve at once.

Mustard To the completed white sauce add 25 g/1 oz (2 tablespoons) butter, 1 tablespoon dry English mustard, 1 tablespoon water and salt and white pepper to taste. Whisk until smooth and creamy and serve with bacon collar (smoked shoulder butt), grilled herrings or flans.

Mushroom To the completed white sauce stir in 225 g/8 oz (2 cups) sliced mushrooms, sautéed in butter.

Apple Sauce

Metric/Imperial	*American*
2 tablespoons water	2 tablespoons water
500 g/1 lb cooking apples	1 lb tart apples
40 g/1½ oz sugar	3 tablespoons sugar
15 g/½ oz butter	1 tablespoon butter
a few drops of lemon juice (optional)	a few drops of lemon juice (optional)

Place the water in a heavy saucepan and heat gently. Peel the apples, quarter and core them and thinly slice into the saucepan. Cover and cook over a very low heat for 10 to 15 minutes until the apples are reduced to a pulp.

Whisk to a fine purée, stir in the sugar, butter and lemon juice and beat well. Serve, hot or cold, with cold meats. Makes about 300 ml/½ pint (1¼ cups).

Apple Sauce; Cranberry Sauce

Cranberry Sauce

Metric/Imperial	*American*
250 g/8 oz fresh cranberries, cleaned	½ lb fresh cranberries, cleaned
6 tablespoons water	6 tablespoons water
125 g/4 oz sugar	½ cup sugar
1 tablespoon shredded orange rind	1 tablespoon shredded orange rind

Place the cranberries in a heavy saucepan with the water. Cover and heat gently. The berries will make popping sounds as they burst their skins.

When all the popping ceases, add the sugar and orange rind to the cranberry pulp and stir over moderate heat until the sugar has dissolved. Spoon into lidded jars or freeze as for apple sauce. Serve with poultry or meats. Makes about 300 ml/½ pint (1¼ cups).

Helpful Hint
Because of the high acid content, Cranberry sauce may be stored in a jam jar at room temperature for 2 to 3 weeks. Both sauces can be frozen in ice cube trays and then released into polythene (plastic) bags and stored in the freezer. Use as required.

Pan Gravy

Metric/Imperial	American
4 tablespoons fat from roasting tin	4 tablespoons fat from roasting pan
600 ml/1 pint hot vegetable water or stock plus meat juices	2½ cups hot vegetable water or stock plus meat juices
1⅓ tablespoons cornflour	1⅓ tablespoons cornstarch

Remove the roast from the tin (pan) and let stand before carving. Pour off all but 4 tablespoons of the fat (drippings).

Dish up the vegetables which accompany your roast, straining them over a large measuring jug so that all the vegetable water is saved. Use water in which strongly flavoured vegetables, such as cabbage, have been cooked, with caution. Add meat juices to this stock to make up to 600 ml/1 pint (2½ cups).

Sprinkle the cornflour (cornstarch) on to the fat in the roasting pan and mix well, stirring to incorporate the sediment in the bottom of the pan. Cook until the flour turns pale brown. Add the vegetable water gradually and bring to the boil, stirring constantly. Transfer to a warmed gravy boat and serve immediately. Makes 600 ml/1 pint (2½ cups) gravy.

Curry Sauce

Metric/Imperial	American
1 tablespoon desiccated or grated fresh coconut	1 tablespoon shredded or grated fresh coconut
120 ml/4 fl oz boiling water	½ cup boiling water
50 g/2 oz margarine	¼ cup margarine
125 g/4 oz diced onion	1 cup diced onion
1 garlic clove, crushed	1 garlic clove, crushed
1 tablespoon curry powder	1 tablespoon curry powder
1 teaspoon curry paste	1 teaspoon curry paste
50 g/2 oz plain white flour	½ cup all-purpose white flour
600 ml/1 pint Chicken Stock (see page 42)	2½ cups Chicken Stock (see page 42)
1 tablespoon lemon juice	1 tablespoon lemon juice
1 tablespoon sugar	1 tablespoon sugar

Place the coconut in a small bowl, pour over the boiling water and let stand for 5 to 10 minutes to infuse.

Melt the margarine and sauté the onions and garlic. Add the curry powder and paste and cook for 3 minutes. Stir in the flour and cook until pale brown. Stir in the stock and bring to the boil. Cover and simmer for 20 minutes.

Press the reserved coconut water through a small sieve (strainer) to extract all the liquid, and add to the sauce, together with the lemon juice and sugar. Heat through and serve. Makes about 750 ml/1¼ pints (3 cups).

Vinaigrette Dressing

Metric/Imperial	American
300 ml/½ pint corn or sunflower oil	1¼ cups corn or sunflower oil
6 tablespoons cider vinegar	6 tablespoons cider vinegar
2 teaspoons salt	2 teaspoons salt
2 teaspoons sugar	2 teaspoons sugar
1 teaspoon black pepper	1 teaspoon black pepper
¼ teaspoon paprika or dry mustard	¼ teaspoon paprika or dry mustard

Place all the ingredients in a large screw-top jar and shake until well mixed. Makes about 400 ml/⅔ pint (1¾ cups).

Apricot Sauce

Metric/Imperial	American
125 g/4 oz dried apricots	⅔ cup dried apricots
strip of lemon rind	strip of lemon rind
50 g/2 oz sugar	¼ cup sugar
150 ml/¼ pint water	⅔ cup water
juice of ½ lemon	juice of ½ lemon

Place the apricots in a bowl with enough water to just cover. Allow to soak overnight.

Next day, place the apricots with the soaking liquid and the lemon rind in a small saucepan over moderate heat. Cook until tender (about 10 to 15 minutes), then rub through a sieve (strainer) to produce a purée.

Dissolve the sugar in the water in a small saucepan over moderate heat, add the lemon juice and bring to the boil. Boil without stirring for 3 minutes. Add the purée and mix well. Serve hot or cold, with sweet or savoury dishes. Makes about 300 ml/½ pint (1¼ cups) sauce.

Orange Sauce

Metric/Imperial	American
2 oranges	2 oranges
50 g/2 oz sugar	¼ cup sugar
300 ml/½ pint water	1¼ cups water
15 g/½ oz arrowroot	2 tablespoons arrowroot

Peel the oranges and carefully remove the white pith, or it will give a bitter taste to the sauce. Place the orange peel in a saucepan with the sugar and water and bring to the boil. Reduce the heat and simmer for 15 minutes.

Meanwhile squeeze the oranges and mix some of the juice with the arrowroot. Reserve the remaining juice.

Remove the peel from the saucepan and return the liquid to the boil. Add the arrowroot and remaining juice and cook for 1 minute, stirring constantly, until the sauce is smooth. Makes about 400 ml/⅔ pint (1⅔ cups).

Meat, Fish and Poultry Dishes

Preparing your own meat dishes and avoiding prepared meals is the sure way of avoiding chemical 'extras'. Stretch expensive red meat with high fibre accompaniments like beans and green vegetables and eat plenty of fish and poultry since, on the whole, these are much lower in fat than red meats.

Spiced Hawaiian Lamb with Limes

Spiced Hawaiian Lamb with Limes

Metric/Imperial	*American*
3 tablespoons oil	3 tablespoons oil
2 onions, sliced	2 onions, sliced
750 g/1½ lb lamb fillet, cubed	1½ lb lamb fillet, cubed
pinch of ground cinnamon	pinch of ground cinnamon
pinch of ground cloves	pinch of ground cloves
2 tablespoons plain flour	2 tablespoons all-purpose flour
300 ml/½ pint pineapple juice	1¼ cups pineapple juice
300 ml/½ pint Chicken Stock (page 42)	1¼ cups Chicken Stock (see page 42)
3 limes or 2 lemons	3 limes or 2 lemons
sprigs of fresh mint or rosemary to garnish	sprigs of fresh mint or rosemary to garnish

Heat the oil and fry the onions gently until tender. Add the cubed lamb and cook over moderate heat until lightly browned on all sides. Stir in the cinnamon, cloves and the flour and cook for 1 minute. Gradually stir in the pineapple juice and chicken stock. Squeeze the juice from 2 of the limes (or 1½ lemons) and add to the pan. Cover and simmer for 30 minutes. Transfer to a casserole, cover and cook in the oven for 40 minutes. Serve garnished with thin slices of the remaining lime or ½ lemon, and small sprigs of mint. Serves 4.

Lamb and Chick Pea Ragoût

Metric/Imperial	American
175 g/6 oz chick peas, soaked in hot water for 4 hours	1 cup chick peas, soaked in hot water for 4 hours
2 onions, sliced	2 onions, sliced
2 tablespoons oil	2 tablespoons oil
1 kg/2¼ lb middle neck of lamb	2¼ lb middle neck of lamb
2 tablespoons plain flour	2 tablespoons all-purpose flour
450 ml/¾ pint Chicken Stock (see page 42)	1¾ cups Chicken Stock (see page 42)
300 ml/½ pint apple juice	1¼ cups apple juice
225 g/8 oz carrots, thinly sliced	2 cups thinly sliced carrots
salt	salt
freshly ground pepper	freshly ground pepper

Drain the chick peas and put into a pan with fresh water to cover. Bring to the boil and simmer for 30 minutes, then drain and reserve.

Meanwhile, fry the onions in the oil until tender. Add the lamb pieces and cook over moderate heat until lightly browned on all sides. Stir in the flour, then gradually add the stock and apple juice. Bring to the boil and add the carrots and salt and pepper. Cover and simmer for 1 hour. Transfer the mixture to a casserole and add the drained chick peas. Cover and cook in a preheated oven (180°C/350°F, Gas Mark 4) for 40 minutes. Serve with a green salad. Serves 4-6.

Hot Pot

Metric/Imperial	American
750 g/1½ lb potatoes, peeled and sliced	1½ lb potatoes, peeled and sliced
1 large onion, chopped	1 large onion, chopped
500 g/1 lb lean minced steak	1 lb lean ground steak
salt	salt
freshly ground pepper	freshly ground pepper
450 ml/¾ pint Beef or Vegetable Stock (see pages 42 and 43)	2 cups Beef or Vegetable Stock (see pages 42 and 43)

Layer the potatoes, onion and meat in a deep earthenware caserole, sprinkling each layer with salt and pepper and ending with a layer of potato.

Pour on the stock, cover and cook in a preheated moderate oven (180°C/350°F, Gas Mark 4) for 2 to 2½ hours. After 1½ hours, stir the casserole to blend all the ingredients together.

Accompany with home-made pickles. Serves 4.

Tender Brisket with Olives

Metric/Imperial	American
3 tablespoons oil	3 tablespoons oil
1-1.25 kg/2-2½ lb beef brisket, rolled and tied	2-2½ lb beef brisket, rolled and tied
salt	salt
freshly ground pepper	freshly ground pepper
1 large onion, chopped	1 large onion, chopped
1 garlic clove, crushed	1 garlic clove, crushed
1 × 400 g/14 oz can tomatoes	1 × 14 oz can tomatoes
175 ml/6 fl oz black olives, stoned	¾ cup pitted ripe olives
150 ml/¼ pint dry white wine	⅔ cup dry white wine
1 teaspoon chopped fresh thyme or ½ teaspoon dried thyme	1 teaspoon chopped fresh thyme or ½ teaspoon dried thyme

Heat the oil in a flameproof casserole. Season the beef well with salt and pepper and put in the casserole. Brown quickly on all sides over high heat. Remove the meat from the casserole and set aside.

Add the onion and garlic to the casserole. Lower the heat and fry gently for 2 to 3 minutes or until golden. Return the meat to the casserole and add the tomatoes, olives, white wine and thyme. Cover the casserole and transfer to a moderate oven (180°C/350°F, Gas Mark 4). Cook for 2 to 2½ hours or until the meat is very tender. Stir a little water into the casserole if it becomes dry during cooking.

Transfer the meat to a hot serving platter and carve into slices. Adjust the seasoning of the sauce and serve separately in a gravy boat. Serve with mashed potatoes and buttered zucchini or green beans. Serves 4-6.

Pork and Beans in Tomato Sauce

Metric/Imperial	American
1 tablespoon oil	1 tablespoon oil
1 large onion, chopped	1 large onion, chopped
1 garlic clove, chopped	1 garlic clove, chopped
500 g/1 lb stewing pork, cut into 2.5 cm/1 inch cubes	1 lb stewing pork, cut into 1 inch cubes
600 ml/1 pint Economical Tomato Sauce (see page 60)	2½ cups Economical Tomato Sauce (see page 60)
1 teaspoon mixed herbs	1 teaspoon mixed herbs
125 g/4 oz button mushrooms, sliced	1 cup sliced button mushrooms
500 g/1 lb haricot beans, cooked (see page 54)	1 lb navy beans, cooked (see page 54)

Heat the oil in a large flameproof casserole and sauté the onions and garlic for 5 minutes until soft but not coloured. Add the meat and sauté for 5 minutes, turning, until browned. Pour over the sauce and herbs, bring to a simmer, cover, then transfer to a preheated moderate oven (180°C/350°F, Gas Mark 4). Cook for 1 hour, until tender.

Remove from the oven and add the mushrooms and cooked beans. Mix well, cover again and return to the oven for 30 minutes more. Serves 6.

Lamb's Liver with Onions

Liver with Onions

Metric/Imperial	American
350 g/12 oz lamb's liver, very thinly sliced	¾ lb lamb's liver, very thinly sliced
2 tablespoons lemon juice	2 tablespoons lemon juice
salt	salt
freshly ground pepper	freshly ground pepper
1 tablespoon chopped parsley	1 tablespoon chopped parsley
2 tablespoons oil	2 tablespoons oil
4 large onions, sliced	4 large onions, sliced

Place the liver slices in a large shallow bowl and pour over the lemon juice, salt and pepper to taste. Mix well, cover with plastic wrap and leave to stand for 1 hour.

Heat the oil in a large frying pan (skillet). In several batches, sauté the liver on both sides for about 1 minute each slice. Drain, transfer the slices to a warmed dish and keep hot. Add the onion to the juices in the frying pan (skillet) and sauté until golden and soft. Transfer to a warmed serving dish and arrange the liver on top.

Garnish with parsley and serve immediately. Serves 4.

Hungarian Fish Casserole

Metric/Imperial	*American*
1 kg/2 lb cod fillet, skinned	2 lb cod fillet, skinned
25 g/1 oz butter	2 tablespoons butter
2 tablespoons oil	2 tablespoons oil
1 onion, sliced	1 onion, sliced
1 garlic clove, crushed	1 garlic clove, crushed
2 tablespoons cornflour	2 tablespoons cornstarch
1 teaspoon paprika pepper	1 teaspoon paprika pepper
1 wineglass dry white wine	1 wineglass dry white wine
1 tablespoon tomato purée	1 tablespoon tomato paste
3 large tomatoes, skinned,	3 large tomatoes, skinned,
seeded and chopped	seeded and chopped
salt	salt
freshly ground pepper	freshly ground pepper

Cut the fish into 5 cm/2 in squares. Heat the butter and oil in a saucepan, add the onion and garlic and cook gently until the onion turns transparent. Add the cornflour (cornstarch) and paprika and cook gently, stirring constantly for 1 minute. Gradually add the wine and bring to the boil, stirring constantly. Reduce the heat, stir in the rest of the ingredients, cover and allow to simmer for 5 minutes.

Transfer to a casserole, cover and cook in a preheated moderate oven (190°C/375°F, Gas Mark 5) for 25 minutes or until heated through, stirring occasionally. Taste and adjust the seasoning. Serves 4 to 6.

Hungarian Fish Casserole

Seafood Pancakes

Metric/Imperial	American
125 g/4 oz plain wholewheat flour	1 cup all-purpose wholewheat flour
salt	salt
freshly ground pepper	freshly ground pepper
2 eggs	2 eggs
250 ml/8 fl oz milk	1 cup milk
1 tablespoon oil	1 tablespoon oil
oil for cooking	oil for cooking
Filling and topping:	*Filling and topping:*
250 g/8 oz cooked white fish, flaked	1⅓ cups flaked cooked white fish
125 g/4 oz peeled prawns	⅔ cup shelled shrimp
3 large tomatoes, skinned and cut into strips	3 large tomatoes, peeled and cut into strips
50 g/2 oz almonds, roughly chopped	½ cup roughly chopped almonds
750 ml/1¼ pints Cheese Sauce (see page 61)	3 cups Cheese Sauce (see page 61)
2 tablespoons finely grated cheese	2 tablespoons finely shredded cheese

For the pancakes, place the flour, salt and pepper in a mixing bowl. In a jug (pitcher) whisk together the eggs, milk and oil. Make a well in the centre of the flour and gradually add the liquid, mixing with a wooden spoon to gradually incorporate the flour in a smooth batter. Allow the mixture to stand for 1 hour before using.

Brush a large frying pan (skillet) with a little oil and heat well over moderate heat. Pour in 2 to 3 tablespoons of batter, and tilt the pan to coat the bottom evenly. Cook until the underside is brown, then turn over and cook the other side. Stack the pancakes on a plate and keep warm.

For the filling, place the fish, prawns (shrimp), tomatoes and nuts in a bowl, add 150 ml/¼ pint (⅓ cup) Cheese Sauce and mix gently. Place 2 tablespoons of filling on each pancake and roll up. Place side by side in a greased shallow ovenproof dish. Pour over the remaining sauce, coating each pancake, and sprinkle with the cheese.

Bake in a preheated moderately hot oven (200°C/400°F, Gas Mark 6) for 20 to 25 minutes until thoroughly heated and golden brown on top. Serve immediately. Serves 4.

Soused Herrings

Metric/Imperial	American
4 medium herrings	4 medium herrings
salt	sea salt and black pepper
freshly ground pepper	1 small onion, finely
1 small onion, finely	chopped
chopped	1 cup white wine vinegar
250 ml/8 fl oz white wine	⅔ cup water
vinegar	6 peppercorns
150 ml/¼ pint water	1 blade mace
6 peppercorns	1 bay leaf
1 blade mace	1 teaspoon light corn syrup
1 bay leaf	
1 teaspoon golden syrup	

Remove the heads from the herrings and scrape off the scales. Clean the fish, keeping them whole, then place, skin uppermost, on a board. Press firmly along the centre of the back of each fish, then turn over and ease away the backbone. Cut off the tails and fins, wash in salted water and dry on paper towels.

Sprinkle the prepared herrings with a little salt and pepper and onion, and roll up from the tail end. Secure with a toothpick (wooden cocktail pick). Pack side by side in a long, narrow dish. Sprinkle with the remaining onion.

Combine the vinegar, water, peppercorns, mace and bay leaf. Season with salt and pepper and pour over the herrings. Spoon over the syrup and cover with foil.

Bake in a preheated moderate oven (180°C/350°F, Gas Mark 4) for 10 to 15 minutes or until the liquid starts to simmer. Reduce the temperature to cool (150°C/300°F, Gas Mark 2) for 1 hour, or until the herrings are a rich dark brown and the liquid has reduced by half. Do not allow the liquid to boil or the herrings will become hard.

Remove from the oven and allow the herrings to become completely cold in the liquid in which they were cooked. Serves 4.

Chicken Curry with Almonds

Metric/Imperial
1 × 1.25 kg/3 lb roast
  chicken
Curry Sauce:
75 g/3 oz grated coconut
450 ml/¾ pint boiling water
2 tablespoons butter
2 large onions, finely
  chopped
1 tablespoon turmeric
1 tablespoon coriander
75 g/3 oz ground almonds
1 teaspoon lemon juice
1 teaspoon mango chutney
1 teaspoon redcurrant jelly
1 teaspoon good curry
  paste
2 teaspoons cornflour
120 ml/4 fl oz natural yogurt
salt
freshly ground pepper

American
1 × 3 lb roast chicken
Curry Sauce:
1 cup shredded coconut
2 cups boiling water
2 tablespoons butter
2 large onions, finely
  chopped
1 tablespoon turmeric
1 tablespoon coriander
¾ cup ground almonds
1 teaspoon lemon juice
1 teaspoon mango chutney
1 teaspoon currant jelly
1 teaspoon good curry
  paste
2 teaspoons cornstarch
½ cup natural yogurt
salt
freshly ground pepper

Cut the chicken meat into bite-sized pieces and arrange in a casserole. To make the sauce, steep the coconut in the boiling water and set aside.

Melt the butter in a large saucepan and sauté the onions over moderate heat for 3 to 5 minutes without browning. Add the turmeric, coriander and almonds and cook for a further 5 minutes. Then add the strained liquid from the coconut, the lemon juice, chutney, redcurrant jelly and curry paste. Bring to the boil, reduce heat and simmer for 20 minutes.

Blend the cornflour (cornstarch) with a little cold water. Stir into the sauce until it has the consistency of single (light) cream. Remove from the heat and stir in the cream. Season with salt and pepper if desired.

Pour the sauce over the prepared chicken, cover and heat through in a preheated moderate oven (180°C/350°F, Gas Mark 4) for 40 minutes. Serve with brown rice and sambals. Serves 6.

Baking

Home-made cakes and biscuits are much better for you than the manufactured varieties, which often contain artificial flavourings and colourings.

In your own kitchen you can keep sugar to the minimum and use sieved wholewheat flours, turning the bran into the bowl after sieving (this contains B vitamins and fibre). Cakes and biscuits made from this type of flour have a slightly heavier texture than the white flour type, but have an excellent flavour.

Chocolate Cake

Spiced Fruit Loaf

Metric/Imperial	American
225 g/8 oz wholewheat self-raising flour	2 cups wholewheat self-rising flour
salt	salt
75 g/3 oz butter	1/3 cup butter
125 g/4 oz mixed dried fruit	3/4 cup mixed dried fruit
50 g/2 oz soft brown sugar	1/3 cup soft brown sugar
1/2 teaspoon mixed spice	1/2 teaspoon all-spice
50 g/2 oz chopped walnuts	1/3 cup chopped walnuts
1 large egg, beaten	1 large egg, beaten
150 ml/1/4 pint milk	2/3 cup milk
demerara sugar	light brown sugar

Sieve the flour with the salt and rub (cut) in the fat, until the mixture resembles fine crumbs. Stir in the fruit, sugar, spice and nuts. Mix with the egg and sufficient milk to give a firm consistency. Pour the mixture into a greased, 450 g/ 1 lb loaf tin (pan) and bake in a preheated moderate oven (180°C/350°F, Gas Mark 4) for 1 1/2 to 2 hours until cooked.

Remove from the oven, sprinkle with sugar and caramelise under a hot grill. Cool in the tin (pan). Makes one 450 g/1 lb loaf.

Chocolate Cake

Metric/Imperial	American
175 g/6 oz wholewheat self-raising flour	1 1/2 cups wholewheat self-rising flour
125 g/4 oz sugar	1/2 cup sugar
175 g/6 oz butter	3/4 cup butter
3 eggs	3 eggs
2 tablespoons cocoa powder, sifted	2 tablespoons unsweetened cocoa, sifted
2 tablespoons boiling water	2 tablespoons boiling water
Topping:	Topping:
75 g/3 oz butter	1/3 cup butter
50 g/2 oz cocoa, sieved	1/2 cup cocoa, sieved
6 tablespoons milk	6 tablespoons milk
225 g/8 oz icing sugar	2 cups confectioner's sugar
8 frosted walnuts	8 frosted walnuts

Brush a 20 cm/8 inch cake tin (pan) with oil and line the bottom with greaseproof (waxed) paper. Place the flour, sugar, butter and cocoa in a large mixing bowl. Add the eggs and beat thoroughly until smooth and creamy. Add the boiling water and beat again. Spoon into the prepared cake tin (pan), level the surface and bake on the middle shelf of a preheated moderate oven (180°C/350°F, Gas Mark 4) for 20 to 30 minutes. When cooked, allow to cool in the tin (pan) for 5 minutes, then turn out on to a wire rack until quite cold.

To make the topping, melt the butter in a small pan, stir in the cocoa and cook gently for 1 minute. Remove the pan from the heat, stir in the milk and icing sugar, mix well to a spreading consistency and use to sandwich the cake together and spread over the top. Decorate with the walnuts. Leave to set. Makes one 20 cm/8 inch cake.

Oat Flapjacks

Metric/Imperial	American
175 g/6 oz wholewheat self-raising flour	1½ cups wholewheat self-rising flour
175 g/6 oz rolled oats or muesli	2 cups rolled oats or müsli
175 g/6 oz sugar	¾ cup sugar
175 g/6 oz margarine or butter	¾ cup margarine or butter
½ teaspoon ground ginger (optional)	½ teaspoon ground ginger (optional)

Lightly oil a 30×23 cm/12×9 inch Swiss roll tin (jelly roll pan).

Place all the ingredients in a mixing bowl, and rub (cut) in the margarine until a stiff dough is formed. Wet your hands and pat the mixture into the prepared tin (pan), level the surface and decorate with the prongs of a fork. Bake in a preheated moderately hot oven (190°C/375°F, Gas Mark 5) for 25 to 30 minutes until just beginning to turn brown.

While still hot, cut into bars with a sharp knife. Cool slightly in the tin (pan), then transfer to a wire rack. When completely cold store in an airtight tin. Makes 16-20 bars.

Granny's Teacake

Granny's Tea Cake

Metric/Imperial	American
350 g/12 oz wholewheat flour	3 cups all-purpose wholewheat flour
1½ teaspoons bicarbonate of soda	1½ teaspoons baking soda
pinch of salt	pinch of salt
1 teaspoon mixed spice	1 teaspoon apple pie spice
½ teaspoon ground cinnamon or grated nutmeg	½ teaspoon ground cinnamon or grated nutmeg
175 g/6 oz butter or margarine	¾ cup butter or margarine
175 g/6 oz demerara sugar	1 cup light brown sugar
175 g/6 oz currants	1 cup currants
100 g/4 oz sultanas	⅔ cup seedless white raisins
300 ml/½ pint milk	1¼ cups milk
grated rind of 1 lemon	grated rind of 1 lemon
2 tablespoons lemon juice	2 tablespoons lemon juice

Grease a 900 g/2 lb loaf tin (pan) and line with greased greaseproof (waxed) paper. Sift the flour, soda, salt and spices into a bowl. Add the butter or margarine and rub (cut) in until the mixture resembles breadcrumbs. Stir in the sugar, currants and sultanas (white raisins). Combine the milk, lemon rind and juice (this will make the milk turn sour and form into clots). Add to the dry ingredients and mix to form a soft dropping consistency. If possible, leave the mixture for a couple of hours.

Turn into the prepared tin (pan), level the top and bake in a moderate oven (160°C/325°F, Gas Mark 3) for 1¾ to 2 hours or until well risen and firm to the touch. Cool in the tin (pan) for 5 minutes before turning on to a wire rack. Wrap in foil or store in an airtight container for 2 to 3 days before use. Makes one 900 g/2 lb loaf.

Oat Slices

Metric/Imperial	American
250 g/8 oz Wholewheat Pastry (see page 92)	½ lb Wholewheat Pastry (see page 92)
4 tablespoons jam	4 tablespoons jam
Filling:	*Filling:*
125 g/4 oz soft margarine	½ cup soft margarine
125 g/4 oz sugar	½ cup sugar
1 teaspoon almond essence	1 teaspoon almond extract
125 g/4 oz jumbo oats	1⅓ cups jumbo oats
3 eggs, beaten	3 eggs, beaten
2 tablespoons flaked almonds, optional	2 tablespoons slivered almonds, optional

Roll out the pastry and line a 30×23 cm/12×9 inch Swiss roll tin (jelly roll pan). Spread with the jam.

Place all the remaining ingredients except the almonds in a large mixing bowl and beat together until smooth. Spoon on to the pastry and spread evenly. Sprinkle with the almonds and bake in a preheated moderately hot oven (190°C/375°F, Gas Mark 5) for 25 to 35 minutes.

Cut into bars with a sharp knife while still hot. Cool slightly in the tin (pan), then transfer the bars to a wire rack until cold. Makes 16-20 bars.

Banana Bread

Metric/Imperial	*American*
125 g/4 oz butter	½ cup butter
125 g/4 oz sugar	½ cup sugar
1 egg	1 egg
250 g/8 oz wholewheat self-raising flour	2 cups wholewheat self-rising flour
½ teaspoon grated nutmeg	½ teaspoon grated nutmeg
500 g/1 lb ripe bananas, peeled	1 lb ripe bananas, peeled
1 teaspoon vanilla extract or a few drops of vanilla essence	few drops of vanilla
75 g/3 oz seedless raisins, tossed in flour	½ cup seedless raisins, tossed in flour
4 tablespoons chopped pecan nuts or walnuts	4 tablespoons chopped pecan nuts or walnuts

Cream the butter and sugar together in a large mixing bowl. Add the egg and mix thoroughly. Sift in the flour and nutmeg, and mix well. Mash the bananas with the vanilla and blend into the mixture. Stir in the raisins and nuts. Pour into a buttered 1 kg/2 lb loaf tin (pan). Bake in a preheated moderate oven (180°C/350°F, Gas Mark 4) for 1 hour or until a skewer inserted in the centre of the cake comes out clean. Cool in the tin (pan) for 5 minutes. Turn out on to a wire rack. Makes one 1 kg/2 lb loaf.

Quick Wholewheat Bread

Metric/Imperial	*American*
375 ml/13 fl oz hand-hot water	1⅔ cups hand-hot water
15 g/½ oz fresh yeast	½ cake compressed yeast
½ teaspoon unrefined sugar	½ teaspoon unrefined sugar
500 g/1 lb wholewheat flour	4 cups wholewheat flour
½ teaspoon salt	½ teaspoon salt

Put one third of the water into a jug and stir in the yeast and ½ teaspoon of the sugar. Leave for about 10 minutes.

Place the flour and salt in a large mixing bowl and add the yeast mixture and remaining water. Mix well to a soft, pliable dough, then tip on to a working surface and knead with your hands for a few minutes, until smooth and no longer sticky. Roll and mould into an oblong to fit one greased 1 kg/2 lb loaf tin (pan). Place in a large plastic bag and fasten the end to protect the dough from draughts and prevent the surface from drying out as the dough rises. Allow the dough to rise in a warm place until it has doubled in size, about 45 to 60 minutes.

Bake the loaf in a preheated moderately hot oven (200°C/400°F, Gas Mark 6) for 35 to 45 minutes. When cooked, the loaf should sound hollow when tapped. Remove from the tin (pan) and cool on a wire rack. Like most brown breads this will not keep for more than 2 days, but freezes very well as soon as it is cold. Makes one 1 kg/2 lb loaf.

Mum's Parkin

Metric/Imperial	American
250 g/8 oz wholewheat self-raising flour	2 cups wholewheat self-rising flour
250 g/8 oz medium oatmeal	1⅓ cups medium oatmeal
250 g/8 oz unrefined sugar	1 cup unrefined sugar
2 teaspoons ground ginger	2 teaspoons ground ginger
2 teaspoons mixed spice	2 teaspoons all-spice
125 g/4 oz margarine	½ cup margarine
250 g/8 oz black treacle	⅔ cup molasses
2 eggs	2 eggs
150 ml/¼ pint milk	⅔ cup milk

Line a deep 20 cm/8 inch spring-release tin (springform pan) with greaseproof (waxed) paper.

Mix the dry ingredients together in a bowl. Melt the margarine and treacle together. Whisk the eggs and milk together in a bowl. Pour the liquids into the dry ingredients and mix to a smooth batter. Pour into the tin (pan) and bake in a preheated moderate oven (160°C/325°F, Gas Mark 3) for 1 hour or until firm. Cool for 15 minutes before turning out on to a wire rack. Best eaten 1 day after baking. Makes one 20 cm/8 inch cake.

Drinks

The variety of commercially produced soft drinks is enormous: from dry powders to which you add your own water or milk, to cans and bottles, squashes and juices. Many of these contain salt and high levels of sugar, but even those without often contain a whole range of colourings, preservatives, emulsifiers and others.

If you want to cut the intake of additives from this area of your diet, try some of our recipes for delicious home-made drinks.

Orangeade

Metric/Imperial	American
2 oranges	2 oranges
50 g/2 oz sugar or clear honey	¼ cup sugar or 4 tablespoons honey
600 ml/1 pint boiling water	2½ cups boiling water

Wash the oranges thoroughly. Grate the rinds carefully with a vegetable grater and squeeze out the juice. Put the rind and juice into a jug with the sugar and pour over the boiling water, stir and leave until cold. Strain and use undiluted. Makes about 750 ml/1¼ pints (3 cups).

Orangeade (Photograph: Summer Orange)

Strawberry Milkshake (Photograph: National Dairy Council)

Fruity Milkshakes

Soft fruits can be used to make marvellous milkshakes. When strawberries or raspberries are in season, purée the fruit in a blender or force through a sieve. Strain the purée, add a little sugar to taste if necessary and freeze in ice cube trays. When required, thaw 3 or 4 ice cubes and stir or whisk into a glass of milk (goats' milk is delicious).

Lemonade

Metric/Imperial
3 large lemons
600-900 ml/1-1½ pints
    cold water
125 g/4 oz clear honey

American
3 large lemons
2½-3¾ cups cold water
⅓ cup honey

Squeeze the lemons and reserve the juice. Place the squeezed lemon shells in a saucepan with the cold water to cover. Bring to the boil, then simmer for 10 minutes. Strain into a jug and add the honey, stirring until dissolved.

Stir in the reserved juice. Taste and add more sugar or honey if desired. Store in the refrigerator and serve hot or cold. Makes about 900 ml/1½ pints (3¾ cups).

Barley Lemonade

Metric/Imperial
50 g/2 oz pearl barley
1.2 litres/2 pints water
strips of lemon rind and
    juice of 2-3 lemons
sugar or honey to taste

American
⅓ cup pearl barley
5 cups water
strips of lemon rind and
    juice of 2-3 lemons
sugar or honey to taste

Wash the barley and put into a heavy saucepan with the water, a pinch of salt and lemon rind. Allow to boil, then simmer slowly for 2 hours. Strain into a large jug.

Strain the lemon juice and add to the barley-water with sugar or honey to taste. Add more lemon juice if desired. Serve hot or cold. Makes about 1.5 litres/2½ pints (6 cups).

Citrus Cooler

Metric/Imperial
500 ml/18 fl oz white grape
    juice
2 tablespoons lemon juice
2 tablespoons orange juice
1 tablespoon sugar

American
2 cups white grape juice
2 tablespoons lemon juice
2 tablespoons orange juice
1 tablespoon sugar

Mix all ingredients together and serve chilled. Serves 4.

Grape Juice and Pineapple Cocktail

Metric/Imperial	American
1 lemon	1 lemon
4 pineapple slices	4 pineapple slices
450 ml/¾ pint white grape juice	1¾ cups white grape juice

Cut 4 thin slices from the lemon and reserve. Squeeze the remaining lemon and strain the juice.

Purée the pineapple in a blender, add the lemon juice, grape juice and honey. Stir and divide between 4 tall glasses, garnishing each with a slice of lemon and adding ice cubes if desired. Serves 4.

Hot Toddy

Metric/Imperial	American
1 egg	1 egg
a little sugar to taste	a little sugar to taste
2-3 tablespoons port or sherry	2-3 tablespoons port or sherry
250 ml/8 fl oz boiling water	1 cup boiling water

Place the egg yolk and sugar in the mug in which the toddy is to be served and whip until light and foamy.

Add the port and fill up with boiling water, stirring all the time. Serve immediately. Serves 1.

Fizzy Lemonade

Metric/Imperial	American
juice of 1 lemon, strained	juice of 1 lemon, strained
300 ml/½ pint cold water	1¼ cups cold water
sugar or clear honey to taste	sugar or honey to taste
½ teaspoon bicarbonate of soda	½ teaspoon baking soda

Mix the lemon juice, water and sugar in a tall glass. Add the soda, stir, and drink while still effervescing. Makes about 350 ml/12 fl oz (1½ cups).

Home-made 'Convenience Foods'

Reducing the number of convenience foods you use because they contain additives need not necessarily mean with-holding the family's favourite foods. Try our home-made Fish Cakes on your children followed by home-made ice cream and chocolate sauce.

Packed full of fresh and nutritious ingredients, the following recipes are among those most commonly bought pre-packed. Our versions are just as tasty as their commercially produced equivalents and are free from all additives and preservatives.

Muesli with Fresh or Dried Fruit

Muesli

Metric/Imperial	*American*
250 g/8 oz rolled oats	2¼ cups rolled oats
125 g/4 oz wheat, rye or barley flakes	4 cups wheat, rye or barley flakes
50 g/2 oz sunflower seeds	⅓ cup sunflower seeds
50 g/2 oz sesame seeds	⅓ cup sesame seeds
125 g/4 oz seedless raisins	⅔ cup seedless raisins
250 g/8 oz mixed dried fruit	1⅓ cups mixed dried fruit
50 g/2 oz cashew or hazelnuts	⅓ cup cashew or hazelnuts

Put all the ingredients into a large bowl, mix well, then store in an airtight container. Makes approximately 850 g/1¾ lb of muesli. About 2 tablespoons per portion, plus some fruit, is ample.

Mayonnaise

Metric/Imperial	*American*
2 egg yolks	2 egg yolks
2 teaspoons dry mustard	2 teaspoons dry mustard
1 teaspoon sugar	1 teaspoon sugar
1 teaspoon salt	1 teaspoon salt
freshly ground pepper	freshly ground pepper
2 teaspoons lemon juice or white wine vinegar	2 teaspoons lemon juice or white wine vinegar
350 ml/12 fl oz corn oil or half corn oil and half olive oil	1½ cups corn oil or half corn oil and half olive oil
1½ tablespoons boiling water	1½ tablespoons boiling water

Start with all the ingredients at room temperature.

Place the egg yolks in a large bowl and whisk for about 2 minutes until creamy. Add the mustard, sugar, salt, pepper and 1 teaspoon lemon juice and beat well to mix thoroughly.

Add the oil, drop by drop, beating constantly until the sauce is thick and smooth.

Add the remaining lemon juice and finally whisk in the boiling water. Transfer to an airtight container and store in the refrigerator. It will keep for 2 to 3 weeks. Makes about 400 ml/⅔ pint (1¾ cups).

Helpful Hint

Mayonnaise is child's play in a blender or food processor. Process all the ingredients except the oil and boiling water for about 1 minute until well combined. With the machine switched on, add the oil at first drop by drop and then in a steady stream through the hole in the lid (or feeder tube). When all the oil has been added the mayonnaise will be ready. Transfer to a bowl and beat in enough boiling water to give a glossy appearance.

Steak and Mushroom Pie

Metric/Imperial	American
1 tablespoon oil	1 tablespoon oil
500 g/1 lb lean braising steak, cubed	1 lb lean braising steak, cubed
1 medium onion, chopped	1 medium onion, chopped
125 g/4 oz mushrooms, chopped or sliced	1 cup chopped or sliced mushrooms
salt	salt
freshly ground pepper	freshly ground pepper
½ teaspoon made mustard	½ teaspoon prepared mustard
600 ml/1 pint Beef Stock (see page 43)	2½ cups Beef Stock (see page 43)
2½ teaspoons vegetarian gravymix	2½ teaspoons vegetarian gravymix
3 teaspoons cornflour	3 teaspoons cornstarch
250 g/8 oz Wholewheat Pastry (see page 92)	½ lb Wholewheat Pastry (see page 92)
beaten egg to glaze (optional)	beaten egg to glaze (optional)

Heat the oil in a large saucepan and sauté the meat cubes until lightly browned. Add the onion, mushrooms, salt and pepper, mustard and stock. Bring to the boil, reduce heat, cover and simmer gently for 1½ hours, or until tender.

Blend the gravymix and cornflour (cornstarch) with a little cold water in a cup and add to the saucepan, stirring constantly over moderate heat until the sauce thickens. Adjust the seasoning and remove from the heat.

Line a 20 cm/8 inch pie dish with just over half the prepared pastry. Spoon in the filling, moistened with a little of the gravy. Dampen the edges of the pastry with water. Roll out the remaining pastry and cover the pie. Press down the edges and flute with a fork. Trim off excess pastry with a sharp knife, and cut pastry leaves from the trimmings to decorate the top.

Glaze with egg if desired and bake on the middle shelf of a preheated moderately hot oven (200°C/400°F, Gas Mark 6) for 30 minutes or until golden. Reheat the remaining gravy and serve separately. Serves 4.

Pork Pie

Metric/Imperial	*American*
Filling:	*Filling:*
500 g/1 lb lean pork, minced or small cubes	1 lb lean pork, minced or small cubes
1 onion, grated	1 onion, grated
½ teaspoon rosemary	½ teaspoon rosemary
½ teaspoon salt	½ teaspoon salt
freshly ground pepper	freshly ground pepper
120 ml/4 fl oz cold water	½ cup cold water
3 soft-boiled eggs, shelled (optional)	3 soft-boiled eggs, shelled (optional)
Hot Water Pastry:	*Hot Water Pastry:*
150 ml/5 fl oz water	⅔ cup water
50 g/2 oz butter	¼ cup butter
250 g/8 oz wholemeal flour	2 cups wholemeal all-purpose flour
¼ teaspoon salt	¼ teaspoon salt

Put the prepared meat, onion, herbs, salt and pepper and water into a bowl and mix well. To make the pastry, put the water and butter into a saucepan and bring to the boil. Sieve the flour and salt. When the water and butter mixture is boiling put all the flour in at once and stir quickly with a wooden spoon. Remove from the heat and mix until the pastry forms a smooth dough.

Tip the dough on to a lightly floured surface and cool slightly. Roll out just over half the pastry thinly, and line a dish (20 cm × 3.5 cm/8 × 1½ inches).

Pile the meat mixture into the lined dish and press it down to level. If using eggs, put them in the dish first then add the meat. Dampen the edge of the pastry with a little water. Roll out the remaining pastry and place on to the pie. Press the edges down. Cut off excess pastry with a sharp knife and flute the edges with a fork. Make a hole in the centre of the pastry and decorate the top with pastry leaves cut from the trimmings. Brush the pie top with beaten egg to give a good glaze and bake in the middle of a preheated moderate oven (350°F/175°C, Gas Mark 4) for 2 to 2½ hours. Turn down the heat if the pastry browns too quickly and cook for a little longer. Serves 4.

Bolognaise Sauce

Bolognaise Sauce

Metric/Imperial	*American*
1 tablespoon oil	1 tablespoon oil
500 g/1 lb minced steak	1 lb minced steak
1 × 400 g/14 oz can tomatoes, chopped	1 × 14 oz can tomatoes, chopped
1 bay leaf	1 bay leaf
2 garlic cloves, crushed	2 garlic cloves, crushed
1 tablespoon tomato purée	1 tablespoon tomato purée
1 teaspoon freshly chopped sweet basil	1 teaspoon freshly chopped sweet basil
salt	salt
freshly ground pepper	freshly ground pepper
150 ml/¼ pint stock	⅔ cup stock

Heat the oil in a large saucepan and gently fry the minced steak. Add all the other ingredients and the stock and stir well. Put the lid on the pan and simmer gently for 1½ hours. Check the stock level occasionally. The sauce should be fairly thick and so boil off surplus liquid if necessary to give a good consistency. Serve with spaghetti or jacket potatoes. Serves 4-6.

Fish Cakes

Metric/Imperial	American
500 g/1 lb white fish, cooked and flaked	1 lb white fish, cooked and flaked
1 bayleaf	1 bayleaf
175 g/6 oz mashed potato	1 cup mashed potato
salt	salt
freshly ground pepper	freshly ground pepper
½ teaspoon prepared mustard	½ teaspoon prepared mustard
1 tablespoon chopped fresh parsley	1 tablespoon chopped fresh parsley
2 teaspoons lemon juice	2 teaspoons lemon juice
1 egg, beaten	1 egg, beaten
For coating:	*For coating:*
½ lb wholemeal flour	2 cups wholemeal flour
1 egg, beaten	1 egg, beaten
150 ml/¼ pint milk	⅔ cup milk
½ lb wholewheat breadcrumbs	4 cups wholewheat breadcrumbs

Poach the fish gently in a little water with the bayleaf for 20 minutes. Drain and cool, then flake. Mix together the fish, potato, egg and seasonings, parsley and lemon juice until smooth.

Place the wholemeal flour on a large plate, and place the breadcrumbs or oatmeal on another. Beat together the egg and milk and pour on to a tray with shallow sides. Tip the fish mixture on to a floured surface and carefully roll into a long thick sausage.

Cut across into 2.5 cm/1 inch slices and pat into neat rounds using a palate knife. Coat the fishcakes one at a time with flour, then dip into the egg and milk mixture and finally coat with breadcrumbs. Place them on a lightly oiled baking sheet.

Deep fry the fishcakes in oil, drain on kitchen paper, and serve immediately with a fresh green salad. Makes about 12 fish cakes.

Variation

To make cheesy fish cakes, halve the quantity of mashed potato and stir in 75 g/3 oz (½ cup) grated cheddar cheese.

Crispy Crunch

Metric/Imperial
125 g/4 oz wheat flakes
125 g/4 oz oat flakes
50 g/2 oz desiccated
   coconut
50 g/2 oz sesame seeds
50 g/2 oz sunflower seeds
25 g/1 oz chopped
   hazelnuts
25 g/1 oz wheatgerm
175 g/6 oz butter
175 g/6 oz golden syrup

American
2 cups wheat flakes
1⅓ cups oat flakes
⅔ cup shredded coconut
⅓ cup sesame seeds
¼ cup sunflower seeds
¼ cup chopped hazelnuts
½ cup wheatgerm
¾ cup butter
½ cup light corn syrup

Lightly oil a 30×23 cm/12×9 inch Swiss roll tin (jelly roll pan). In a large bowl, combine the wheat and oat flakes, coconut, seeds, nuts and wheatgerm. Melt the butter with the syrup in a heavy saucepan over low heat. Add to the dry ingredients and mix to a tacky mixture.

With wet hands, press the mixture into the prepared tin (pan) and bake in a preheated moderate oven (180°C/350°F, Gas Mark 4) for 15 to 20 minutes.

Cut into squares with a sharp knife while still hot. Cool slightly in the tin (pan), then transfer the squares to a wire rack until cold. Store in an airtight tin. Makes about 18 squares.

Wholewheat Pastry

Metric/Imperial
500 g/1 lb wholewheat flour
¼ teaspoon salt
250 g/8 oz firm margarine
   or butter, in small pieces
1 teaspoon lemon juice
   mixed with 7
   tablespoons cold water

American
4 cups wholewheat flour
¼ teaspoon salt
½ cup firm margarine or
   butter, in small pieces
1 teaspoon lemon juice
   mixed with 7
   tablespoons cold water

Sift the flour into a large mixing bowl. Add the salt, if using. Rub (cut) in the fat until the mixture resembles fine breadcrumbs.

Make a well in the centre and pour in most of the water and lemon juice. Mix together lightly to a pliable, non-sticky dough. Use the rest of the water if necessary (wholewheat flour needs a little more water than white flour to render it pliable).

Knead gently on a working surface for a few seconds until smooth. Use immediately or rest in refrigerator until required. Alternatively, freeze for future use. Makes 750 g/1½ lb pastry.

Home-made Ice Cream

Metric/Imperial	American
4 large eggs, separated	4 large eggs, separated
50 g/2 oz castor sugar to taste	¼ cup sugar to taste
2 teaspoons vanilla essence	2 teaspoons vanilla
300 ml/½ pint double cream	1¼ cups heavy cream

Whisk the egg whites in a bowl until stiff and glossy. Add the sugar a tablespoon at a time, whisking well between each addition, to make a stiff meringue mixture. Cover the bowl with plastic wrap and set aside.

Mix the vanilla with the egg yolks, then swiftly whisk the yolks into the meringue mixture to an even golden colour.

Whip the cream in a large bowl until quite thick and fold in the meringue mixture, using a large metal spoon.

Pour the ice cream mixture into a 1 kg/2 lb loaf tin (pan) lined with foil, level the surface and freeze. When frozen, the block of ice cream may be tipped out of the tin (pan) and returned to the freezer in a sealed heavy-duty plastic bag. It will freeze for up to 2 months. When required, transfer the ice cream to a serving plate and allow to rest in the refrigerator for 30 minutes before serving. Makes 12 portions.

Variations

Strawberry When part-frozen, mash 225 g/8 oz (1½ cups) puréed strawberries into the Ice Cream.

Peach Add 225 g/8 oz (1½ cups) fresh peaches as above.

Home-made Ice Cream (page 93) with Chocolate Sauce

Chocolate Sauce

Metric/Imperial	American
2 tablespoons cocoa powder	2 tablespoons unsweetened cocoa
2 tablespoons golden syrup	2 tablespoons light corn syrup
2 tablespoons cold water	2 tablespoons cold water

Place all the ingredients in a heavy saucepan and heat gently over moderate heat, stirring constantly, until the sauce is smooth and glossy. Serve hot or cold on ice cream, poached pears, bananas or meringues. (When cooled, the sauce will thicken slightly.) Makes 90 ml/3 fl oz (6 tablespoons).

Index

Additives 4-21
Allergies 9-14
Anti-oxidants 4, 18-19
Apple sauce 62
Apples, poached 32
Apricot sauce 65
Apricots, poached 32
Avocados with shellfish 41
Banana bread 80
Barbecue sauce 60
Barley lemonade 84
Béchamel sauce 61
Beef:
    Beef stock 43
    Bolognaise sauce 90
    Hot pot 68
    Tender brisket with olives 68
Beetroot in soured cream 49
Bolognaise sauce 90
Bran teabread 34
Broad bean and green pea
    casserole 55
Broccoli, stir-fried 48
Brown rice pilaff 52
Brown rice stuffed tomatoes
    40
Butter bean bake 56
Butter bean salad 53
Cabbage in white sauce 46
Cancer 12, 13
Carbohydrates 22
Carotene 5
Celery crunch 48
Cereals 26, 28
Cheese 24; sauce 61
Cherries, poached 32
Chicken curry with almonds 74
Chicken stock 42
Chocolate cake 76
Chocolate sauce 94
Citrus cooler 84
Colourings 5, 8, 10, 14, 15, 16
Cottage cheese and date
    starter 39
Cranberry sauce 62
Crispy crunch 92
Cucumber stuffed tomatoes
    40
Curry sauce 64

Dietary fibre 22, 28
Dried fruit 27, 28; compote 30
Drinks and liquids 29
Eggs 24-5
Emulsifiers 5, 14, 15, 19-21
Fats and oils 22, 29
Fish 23-4:
    Fish cakes 91
    Hungarian fish casserole 71
Flapjacks 77
Flavourings 29; artificial 5, 14,
    15
French beans with bacon 50
Fresh foods 22-5
Fruit 25. *See also* Apple etc.
    Fruit breakfasts 30-3
    Fruity milkshakes 83
    Poached fruit 32-3
Garlic croûtons 49
Gnocchi alla Romana 58
Granny's tea cake 78
Granola 37
Grape juice and pineapple
    cocktail 85
Gravy in pan 63
Greengages, poached 32
Herbs, dried 28-9
Herrings, soused 73
Hot toddy 85
Hyperactivity 9, 12
Ice cream, home-made 93
Insecticides and sprays 8, 11
Kidney bean casserole 55
Lamb:
    Lamb and chick pea ragoût
        67
    Spiced Hawaiian lamb with
        limes 66
Lecithins 5, 19
Leek and celery soup 45
Lemonade 84; fizzy 85
Liver with onions 70
Malt bread 36
Mayonnaise 87
Meat 23. *See* Beef, Lamb etc.
Milk 24
Milkshakes, fruity 83
Minerals 22
Molluscs 24

Monosodium glutamate 4, 10, 13-14
Muesli 86
Mushroom sauce 61
Mushroom soup 44
Mushrooms, marinated 38
Mustard sauce 61
Nitrates, nitrites 4, 10, 11, 13
Nucleotides 6
Nuts and kernels 27, 29
Oat slices 79
Offal 23
Orange and banana starter 33
Orange bread 36
Orange sauce 65
Orangeade 82
Parkin 81
Parsley sauce 61
Pasta 56-8
Plums, poached 32
Pork and beans in tomato sauce 69
Pork pie 89
Preservatives 4, 12, 15, 17-18
Proteins 22
Prunes, compote of 31
Pulses 27-8, 29, 54-6
Ratatouille 47
Salt 6
Sauces 59-65, 90, 94
Scotch broth 44

Seafood pancakes 72
Shellfish 24; avocados with 41
Spiced fruit loaf 76
Spices 29
Spinach gnocchi 58
Spreads 29
Stabilizers 4, 19-21
Steak and mushroom pie 88
Stocks 42-3
Storecupboard 26-9
Strawberry smoothie 33
Sugar and sweeteners 29
Sunshine salad 52
Tartrazine 4, 8, 10, 12, 16
Tea bread 34
Tomato:
    Brown rice stuffed tomatoes 40
    Cucumber stuffed tomatoes 40
    Tomato sauces 57, 60
Vegetable medley 51
Vegetable stock 42
Vegetables 25
Vinaigrette dressing 64
Vitamins 22
White sauce 61
Wholewheat bread, quick 80
Wholewheat pastry 92
Wholewheat scones 35

The publishers would like to thank the following photographers:
Bryce Attwell 23, 78, 94; Robert Estall 11 above; Robert Golden 38, 47,54, 59; Melvin Grey 50, 66; Robert Harding/Picture Library/Walter Rawlings 6; Gina Harris 2-3, 70; Paul Kemp 31, 43, 51, 62, 71, 75, 90; Roger Phillips 22, 26, 27, 35, 86; The Photographers' Library 7, 11 below.

Monosodium glutamate, 21
11
Mousse, 60
Mushroom sauce, 61
Mushroom soup, 21
Mushrooms, marinated, 43
Mustard sauce, 61
Nitrates, nitrites in cured meats
Nucleic acids, 21
Nuts and kernels, 21
Oatmeal, 29
Oil, 127
Orange and beet salad
Oranges, 126, 130
Oranges
Orangeade, 29
Panar, 81
Parsley, chopped
Pasta, 36, 39
Pastry, poached
Peas and beans, 21, 131
Peppers, 61
Pernod, 63
Pickles, 21, 131
Potatoes, 21
Prunes, compote of
Pulses, 21, 131
Ratatouille, 43
Salad, 131
Sauces, 60-61
Scotch broth, 16

Second remedies, 72
Shellfish, raw, 130, 131, 141
Spiced fruit loaf, 16
Sugar, 29

The publishers would like to thank the following for their pictures:
Bryce Attwell 73, 89; Robert Estall 63, 111; Laurie Evans/Robert Golden
37; Melvin Grey 71; Robert Harding Association/Library Waters, 54-55;
Gina Harris 34; Robert Harding 31, 65, 77, 93, 97; Paul Kemp/Philip
22, 26, 27, 35, 85; The Photographers' Library 7, 11 below.